ANGLING

IN

THE KUMAUN LAKES

ANGLING
IN
THE KUMAUN LAKES.

WITH A MAP
OF
THE KUMAUN LAKE COUNTRY.

BY
W. WALKER, M. D.

GYAN

Published by

Gyan Publishing House
5, Ansari Road
Daryaganj, New Delhi-110002
Phone: 011-47034999, 9811692060
E-mail: books@gyanbooks.com

Distribution Network
gyanbooks.com
India, USA, Canada, UK, Australia, France

ISBN: 978-81-212-7941-3 (PB)
First Published, 1888

2nd Impression 2023

Printed at: Gyan Press, Delhi.

ANGLING IN THE KUMAUN LAKES
Author: W. WALKER

ANGLING

IN

THE KUMAUN LAKES.

WITH A MAP

OF

THE KUMAUN LAKE COUNTRY.

BY

W. WALKER, M.D.

CALCUTTA
THACKER, SPINK AND CO.

1888.

PREFACE.

DEAR READER,—As I have a great desire to see you quit this land of your exile in as sound health as you stepped on the shores of India, I have written this little book to tempt you out into the bright sun-light on the rippling waters of the Kumaun Lakes, instead of spending your hard-won holiday on the social tread-mill of a hill-station. If I succeed, I shall have induced to share with me a real "elixir vitæ," which will help you safe home to a green old age by the "ingle neuk" of your boyhood.

W. W.

CONTENTS.

CHAPTER I. — PAGE.

INTRODUCTORY 1

CHAPTER II.

NAINI-TAL 9

CHAPTER III.

BHIM-TAL 40

CHAPTER IV.

NAUKUCHIA-TAL 61

CHAPTER V.

MALWA-TAL 75

CHAPTER VI.

SATH-TAL 90

ANGLING

IN

THE KUMAUN LAKES.

CHAPTER I.

INTRODUCTORY.

"Away, then away,
We lose sport by delay:
First leave all our sorrows behind us:
If Miss Fortune should come,
We are all gone from home:
And a-fishing she never can find us."

HAVING often been asked by personal friends to give them the benefit of my experiences of angling in the lakes of Kumaun, I am induced, during a season of enforced leisure, to string together a few notes which may in future years help a brother Angler to add to the weight of his basket, while he shakes off the cares of official work and the dreadful lassitude of the plains by a few weeks' ramble in the Himalayan lake country.

Europeans have scarcely yet begun to realize that, while sweltering in the Courts of Agra, Allahabad or Benares, soul and body at the point of giving way to the depressing influences of work and climate, they are actually within a few hours' journey of splendid sport in a charming climate, amidst some of the loveliest scenery in the world, to which they can flee away from the dust and the heat and the weary monotony of hot-weather life in the plains, and

> "All the pleasures prove, that valleys, groves
> or hills or field,
> Or woods and steepy mountains yield."

Besides accessibility, the lake region of Kumaun has one other great advantage over most angling resorts in India; its climate is invigorating and health restoring. The lakes almost all lie at a considerable elevation, 4,000 to 6,400 ft. above the sea-level, and even when the heat of the sun's rays must be acknowledged to be tropical, the temperature in the shade is only a genial warmth, and the exertion required in angling from a boat is so trifling in comparison to that involved in fishing on the banks of any river, that the most shaky victim of work may safely engage in it. In fact, there could, in my opinion, be no more happy combination suggested of sport with gentle exercise in the open air, nor any so well suited to recall elasticity of mind and body to a jaded victim of office work.

It is an odd reflection that the lakes to which I am inviting all honest anglers, as to a house of refuge from the exhausting effects of an Indian climate, should be the direct result of the action of ice at a period of the world's history when the slopes of the Himalayan ranges were being ground and torn by glaciers and ice-fields. That this was the case no one can doubt who has studied the position, the configuration, and the surroundings of the Kumaun lakes, having in his hands the notes of Mr. Theobald of the Geological Survey. The lakes are eight in number, and may be divided, from the angler's point of view, into those that are worth fishing and those that are not. In the first group I include—

1. Naini-tal.
2. Bhim-tal.
3. Sath-tal.
4. Naukuchia-tal.
5. Malwa-tal.

and in the second group—

6. Suria-tal.
7. Khurpa-tal.
8. An unnamed lake above the last.

"The origin of all these lakes is," says Mr. Theobald, "identical, and, putting aside all considerations of rock basins which I have no means of verifying, is due to the obstruction of local drainage caused by the debris of old moraines on the retrocession of the glaciers at the termination of the glacial epoch." Granting that several of the lakes occupy in parts of their areas ice-cut basins, a postulate which Mr. Theobald does not question, there is no difficulty in determining in all the lakes the position and remains of the old moraines, which are the chief cause of the existence of the lakes as permanent sheets of water.

But I hasten to leave disputed ground. The site of an old moraine is too fruitful of awkward missiles to suit the taste of a gentle angler, when caught between irate geologists. Under whatever conditions the lakes were produced, *there they are:*—and our present purpose is to catch the fish that dream away their lives in their deeps and sport in their shallows.

The converging point for all travellers to the

Kumaun lakes is the Katgodam station of the Bareilly and Kumaun Railway. Stepping out of the train, were it not for the rabble of besieging coolies, the eager sportsman might hear, as he stands on the platform, the subdued sound of the Gola river as it rushes over its boulder bed a few hundred yards to the east of the station. This small river receives in its course from Malwa-tal, where it rises, to the Bhabar canals, in which it is practically lost, the surplus waters of Naini-tal, Bhim-tal, Sath-tal and Naukuchia-tal; and as there is now no obstruction at its exit from Malwa-tal to the passage of large fish, it is a stream that might be well stocked with Mahsir and Baril, were steady pressure exercised to prevent netting. Some years ago efforts were made to check the use of nets, and I had the satisfaction of having one or two good afternoons' sport in the stretch of water between the iron bridge, close to the Katgodam station and the Rani-bagh dâk bungalow. Vigilance was, however, again relaxed, and in one season the river was emptied of fish. Now, again, I hear that the present Commissioner, himself a keen fisherman, is doing what he can to prevent wholesale destruction of the fish, and it is quite worth the while of a keen fisherman (who has no reason to be afraid of the sun) arriving at Katgodam any time during the months of April, May and the first half of June, or again during the latter half of September and the whole of October, to devote twenty-four hours to this small river. There is a fairly well managed Hotel close to the Railway station.

Near the iron suspension bridge you will find a temporary weir, which leads the water into the Eastern Bhabar canals, and in the long pool above this weir some pretty fly-fishing may be had. In fishing the Gola you must be prepared to wade, crossing and recrossing the stream as the configuration of the banks demands. About a quarter of a mile above the suspension bridge, there is another temporary weir, which diverts the water into the canal that passes through Haldwani and so on to the Western Bhabar irrigation: and in the pool above this weir there are always a few good fish, and many small ones, to be found. Both these weir-pools must be fished by wading quietly down from above, keeping as near mid-stream as possible and casting well under the bank on both sides. The biggest fish will be killed on the small gold fly-spoon, but, especially towards evening, any dark colored fly with a claret body and mixed wing will bring to bank many fish averaging over a pound in weight. As the fish are easily disturbed in these pools, you must hold hard those which you hook, and prevent them from passing down the pool to frighten the others.

It is useless, in my experience, to fish very early or very late in the Gola. Even in the hottest months a chill wind blows down the valley (the "Dadu") until the sun is well up, and the same wind is again strong on the water before the last rays of the sun have ceased to gild the higher hill tops. My advice therefore is to begin to fish when the sun is well up, and to give up at 11 A. M., beginning again as soon as the shadows of the western hills are touching the water.

Between the upper weir - pool and the gorge below the Rani-bagh bungalow, a distance of about a mile, there is not much deep water, but there are many runs that ought to hold good fish under favourable circumstances. In the gorge itself there are a few deep rushes under overhanging rocks, and out of these I have taken fish weighing up to 10 lbs, using the small gold spoon. To reach these rapids a good deal of rough clambering has to be done; and a fish when hooked on fine gut must be humoured and coaxed into quiet back waters, if he is to be bagged.

The waters of the Gola above Rani-bagh do not, under existing conditions, repay the toil and inconvenience endured in fishing them. The banks are difficult, and at those periods of the year when the fishing is likely to be really good, the sun strikes viciously down into the narrow valley, driving even lizards to the shelter of the rocks. I have fished this portion of the river both in May and in September, and never found the sport compensate for the labor and the grilling.

Having given up twenty-four hours to the Gola, we may now pass on to the lakes whose waters feed that river. If the visit be made early in the season, that is between the 1st March and the 15th April, I strongly advise the fly-fisher to devote a week to Naini-tal. From Katgodam to the Brewery is a lovely Tonga-drive of three hours; and a ride of one hour further will take the visitor to one or other of the hotels. Boats and boatmen are easily procurable in early spring, and the earlier the visit is paid the more successful is the sport likely to be.

CHAPTER II.

Naini-tal.

According to the N. W. P. Gazetteer, compiled by Mr. E. T. Atkinson, c. s., the greatest length of the Naini lake is 4,703 feet, the maximum breadth 1,518 feet, and the elevation of the surface at flood-level about 6,410 feet above the sea. It occupies the bottom of a valley which runs about north-west, south-east. Overlooking the valley are the high peaks of China (8,568′), Lyria Kanta (8,144′), Dio-patha (7,989′) and Ayar-patha (7,721′).

Fly-fishing on Naini-tal has of late years become discredited; and I am forced to confess that during the season, say from the 1st May till the weather becomes in October too cold for fly-fishing, it is with considerable difficulty and with the exercise of much patience and skill that a fish can be got to rise to a fly. One may count the mahsir in hundreds basking on the surface, or lazily rolling themselves porpoise-like in the glittering wavelets, or anon rushing madly after minnows, but the fly - fisher will drop his fly in vain near them.

Several causes have combined to produce this result. First, as old Izaak said about the carp, a very near relative of the mahsir, "he is a very subtle fish and hard to be caught." This fact will be accepted with some difficulty by men who have fished for the mahsir only in solitary, unfrequented rivers, where the shadow of a rod, flits across the runs and pools once or twice in a year. Under such circumstances there is no bolder fish swims than the mahsir; and the biggest fish at the top of the pool will lead the dance of death merrily for half a dozen of his companions before the shoal takes fright at the splashing and awkward gambols of the most inexperienced fisherman. It is otherwise with the mahsir reared in the Naini lake. These fish are rarely found far out from the weeds which border the lake and which rise to the surface from varying depths of six to sixteen feet. Their holds are in these weeds, and there they find abundance of food. Unfortunately for the angler the outer edge of the fringe of weeds is precisely the most fascinating lounge for the unfeathered bipeds who seek their pleasure on the lake. There they enjoy the *dolce far niente* of the water, while they can at the same time see and be seen by the frequenters of the mall. This is one ever present cause of disturbance to the fish. But there is another far more aggravating source of trouble to the fly-fisher, namely, the troller. For many years trolling along the edge of the weeds was by the common consent of all anglers on the lake avoided; but lately this form of sport has been specially patronized by the Municipal Committee; and every season, two or three men appear on the scene who find sport in being rowed round the lake for hours at a time, a long line trailing for thirty yards behind their boats, in the hope of a run. A few fish are caught in this way, many more are cut, while the rest are so alarmed that for some hours after the passage of a troller not a fish will rise to the fly.

Many a time and often I have found myself at the windward end of a long patch of weeds, dropping gently down with a lovely curl on the water, the fish rising at the fly on every yard, when all of a sudden the rise ceases, every fish disappears and a sound drifts along the lake like the beat of the paddles of a Mississippi steamer. Presently you will be introduced to the Naini-tal troller. Lying back comfortably in the stern of his barge, a stalwart Kamauni laboring with rythmical beat at the weary oar, clouds of smoke rising from his well-colored meerschaum, the troller seems to enjoy his sport such as it is; but it never seems to dawn upon him in the faintest degree that he is selfishly spoiling the sport of every fly-fisher on the Lake. I have no fault to find with the troller in his proper place, say at Tangrot or on the Raiwala pool; but on the Naini lake he is as much out of place and commits as great an offence against the comity of sport, as the man who would shoot a pig on ground sacred to the Meerut Tent Club; and I hope that the next time a troller mars a fly-fisher's sport on Naini-tal, he may meet the fate of Hiawatha when he went afishing for the great Mishe-nahma.

But notwithstanding these troubles and difficulties, the wily mahsir may be bagged even on the Naini lake; but before describing when, where and how, let me give you a few hints as to the rod and tackle and the mode of fishing which I recommend for adoption on all the Kumaun lakes. Premising that, unless for bank fishing, a boat is necessary, and that a boat is seen by the fish a very long way off, and heard still farther, my advice is to choose a small boat, and to insist on the oars being well muffled, and that the boatman shall paddle you silently stern foremost at such a distance from the outer fringe of weeds as will admit of your landing your fly uniformly, at the end of a straight cast, on the outer edge of the weeds. Indeed, if you can only make sure of not hooking the weeds, the most deadly cast of all is to drop your fly on the weeds, and to draw it slowly and quietly off them into deep water. Here, if anywhere, your fishing to be successful must be "fine and far off," and you should, under all circumstances, aim at making your cast at right angles to the line of the weeds. You will often be tempted by the breeze blowing up or down the lake to throw the fly in front of you; but much experience has convinced me that this is a mistake. Not only are you placed at a disadvantage in hooking a rising fish by the slackening of your line in the forward motion of the boat, but as the fish lie watching in the weeds, a fly dropt from a cast at right angles to them moves away in a straight line, covering as it were the retreat of the casting line, and a fish in pursuit of the fly does not see the cast until it is too late. Whereas, when a cast is made obliquely along the edge of the weeds, a fish darting at the fly cannot fail to see the casting line on his attempt to intercept the retreating insect; and so well educated is the Naini fish to the meaning of a piece of gut, that he will at once stop in his rush and turn back with a lordly sweep of his broad tail, and seek the glades of the weed forest with supreme contempt for such bungling.

One other word of advice I have to give which is applicable to all lake fishing is, never to fish with the sun behind you. Under such circumstances the shadow of your rod or of your line will assuredly telegraph a warning to the fish, and not a fin will move. The only exception allowable to this rule may be when there is a strong breeze blowing and the turmoil of the water is sufficient to blur the shadows. But even then I would prefer to fish in the sun's eye, and would feel sure that my fishing would be more successful.

To enable you to throw out neatly and well a long straight line you must use a double-handed rod; but it need be neither very long nor very heavy. A 14 feet green heart rod, with the top made rather stiff, and some flexibility to within three feet of the butt, and with standing rings, is the description of rod which I have used for many years. With such a rod you can readily lift a long line out of the water, and as you are rarely called upon to use the finest tackle, there is not much danger of flicking your flies off. For a running line I always use 60 to 80 yards of strong plaited silk line; and I have known every yard of it required before a vigorous fish tired himself in his first rush. I allow myself always 12 or 13 feet of casting line; from the loop for four feet it should be of tapering twisted double gut; then three feet of the best salmon gut with a large loop cast on it; then three or four feet of strong trout gut, finishing off with three feet of medium or fine trout gut according to the circumstances of the hour. As the evening falls, or should the wind rise, I am in the habit of removing the lighter gut, shifting my fly to the stronger part of the cast and *vice versâ*. Should I resolve to try a small gold-spoon or fly minnow, I can at once remove the lighter gut, and attach its trace to the large loop of the single salmon gut strands.

These precautions are advisable because at any moment you may find yourself struggling with an active fish of 7 or 8 lbs., and it is folly to use finer tackle than the circumstances of the water and of the hour demand. It is, however, surprising how much sport one may get in Naini-tal if reckless of the loss of tackle. One evening I was challenged by an intelligent 'banker' to throw a fly over a fish of ten or twelve pounds' weight lazily floating near the surface in front of his pitch. The face of the lake was like the surface of a mirror, and not a breath was stirring.

Putting down my large rod, I took up a 10-feet fly rod that was in my boat, and shaking out the fine drawn gut casting line with a small grey midge on it, I made a few casts and then dropt the midge just behind the eye of the monster. He turned slowly round, sailed up to the fly, and in a second I had the No. 17 hook fixed in his leathery mouth. Off he went to the deeps, and I watched with anxiety yard after yard of my line disappearing. Alas ! there was no check to his excursion, for the gut parted as he exhausted the line. At other times I have had under similar circumstances much better fortune, landing fish of five and six pounds on the finest gut (natural, not drawn) that Farlow could send me.

As I shall have so often to allude to the dense fringe of weeds that frames the waters of Naini-tal, I may as well here transcribe from the N. W. P. Gazetteer the botanical nomenclature of the plants which compose it. Mixed together in a tangled mass, there are potomageton micronatum, myrophyllum Indicum, chara verticillata, polygonum scabrinervium, "and the pretty English polygonum amphibium, which according to Madden, here and here only in India, raises its pink spikes above the water." As an angler I wish much that the "pretty English Polygonum" had betaken himself elsewhere, for his "lovely spikes" are the most stubborn things that a hook can lay hold of: they object most strongly to all reasonable treatment at a distance, and insist on a personal interview before they will consent to let go their hold. The stems moreover are as tough as Rhœa grass.

I may here also note the species of fish which I have caught or seen caught in the Naini lake. Numbers 1, 2 and 4 rise to the fly; the others are purely ground feeders. I am indebted to the kindness of the Curator of the Indian Museum, Calcutta, for the identification of numbers 2, 5 and 6.

(1) Barbus Tor (The Mahsir).

(2) Barbus Chilinoides (the lake fish) or "Kali Macchi."

(3) Barbus Conchonius.

(4) Barilius Bola (Hill trout).

(5) Ophiocephalus Gachua (Murrel).

(6) Orcinus Sinuatus (Risala).

In the early part of the season, when the lake is not much disturbed by pleasure-seekers, the best plan is to begin fishing about 3 P.M., under the shadow of Ayar patha, near the Hindu temple at the west end of the lake, working slowly to the eastward and fishing carefully every yard of the water. In front of the temple very large fish often congregate in numbers: but being an honest angler, you will listen to Martial and forbear from tempting them—

> "Piscator, fuge: ne nocens recedas,
> Sacris piscibus hæ natantur undæ."

After trying a very large assortment of flies on the Naini water, I have arrived at the conclusion that there are four flies which will stir any fish, if he is in the humour, and I now rarely trouble myself to go outside these for varieties. Premising that for lake fishing no fly need be dressed on a larger hook than a No. 6 or No. 5 of the Limerick or Pennell-Limerick bend, and that I give unqualified preference to the down-eyed hooks, because there is no attached gut loop to rot and betray your confidence at a critical moment, I will here describe the flies with which I have done most work.

First, the "Yellow Spider." Tag gold tinsel; but peacock harl; body of yellow floss with three turns of fine gold thread: a very full shoulder hackle of mallard feathers dyed canary; head of black ostrich tag; a couple of fibres of peacock harl for antennæ. This fly (save the mark!) has no wings and no tail, and it appears to me to resemble nothing so much as a yellow spider in the water. Whatever the mahsir may take it for, it is undoubtedly at all seasons a very fascinating lure for all fish under ten pounds.

Second, the "Claret Fly." Tag gold tinsel; tail golden pheasant topping; but yellow floss with turn of gold tinsel; body claret floss merging into dark brown or black towards the shoulder;

gold thread : thin claret hackle on body with a full jay hackle for legs ; wings a mixture of slips of dark turkey, bustard, golden pheasant tippet, and dark teal ; head black.

Third, the "Silver Doctor."

Fourth, "Jock Scott."

If one or other of these four flies does not tempt the fish to rise, you may rest assured that they are not in the humour.

I have caught a few good fish in the Naini lake with the small gold fly-spoon : but it is not usually so successful a lure as it is in rivers. And here I may as well describe the fly-spoon which I have been in the habit of using for the past twenty years, and which I consider perfection for general sport using a fly rod and light tackle.

The spoons are made for me by one 'Mooni' Misteri residing in the Bareilly city, but any sharp worker in metal can make them, provided he knows how to electro-plate. I have them made of two sizes, pear shaped in outline, and almost quite flat. The larger measures two inches in length, and $1\frac{1}{8}''$ at its widest part, and weighs considerably less than half a tolah ; the smaller measures $1\frac{5}{8}''$ in length and $\frac{7}{8}''$ at its widest part, and weighs only a quarter of a tolah. The metal of which the spoons are made is so thin that they can be bent and unbent with great ease, according as the current in which they are being worked is slack or strong. They are as easily thrown as a large salmon fly, and by a little management and skill can be made to spin the moment they touch the water. Their action in spinning is so smooth and easy that I have never known my fly rod injured by it; and working as the spoons do only two or three inches beneath the surface, there is no drag on the top joint in lifting them out of the water for a fresh cast.

The mounting of these spoons is very simple. I don't believe in tail hooks to a spoon bait, but invariably trim the flight of triplets from the head of the spoon. The flight itself consists of three triplets, of small size, but of stout build. The uppermost triplet should be metal-eyed, the second and third plain: all three should be strongly whipped, and the middle triplet knotted as well, to a strong piece of double or treble gut lightly twisted. The uppermost hook is fastened by its eye to the split ring or copper wire which forms the connexion between the spoon and the first swivel, and it rests close under the head of the spoon. The middle triplet should be attached about two-thirds down the length of the spoon and the lowermost so as to have the top of its shank a line or a line and a half beyond the lower edge of the spoon.

For the attachment of the first swivel of the

trace to the spoon and to the flight of hooks, there is a convenience in using a split ring. I have once or twice succeeded in getting split rings that I could trust, but this is a difficult matter; and unless you have unlimited confidence in the steel of which the rings are made, I recommend a neat fastening of copper wire. Many a time and oft have I lost my spoon and flight of hooks from misplaced confidence in a split ring; sometimes a badly tempered ring snaps clean across; sometimes the ring fails to close, and the eye of the swivel insinuates itself into the split and gradually works itself free; or again, the ring will straighten out as if made of soft iron, and set the swivel free. Hence I recommend a copper wire fastening.

While writing of the fly-spoon I may as well place on record an observation which has forced upon me the conclusion that it is a mistake to "belly" a spoon or to give it what is called a "hogback." No doubt a spoon thus made will spin well, but it always will spin *on its own axis*. The thing looks lively enough in the water, but it has no resemblance to any living creature that swims; not even the most dissipated Chilwa or Baril was ever seen rollicking along at such a pace. The difference between this wild whirl through the water and the motion of a flat spoon slightly bent is so marked and so distinctive that it may well account for the success of the flat fly-spoon as a lure. I have often studied the motion of one of these fly-spoons from the high bank above a pool where another fisherman was at work, and have been struck with the fact that unless in the heaviest water, it spins not *on its own axis* but *on the axis of the trace*, and while thus spinning, it produces an optical delusion which presents the spoon and the flight of hooks, exactly like a large yellow moth, struggling through the water with its legs depending from its body. I sketch below the phantom as seen from above, and I know of no reason why the same delusion should not be presented to the fish looking from below.

The traces for these spoons I make always of single gut: of the very best and strongest salmon gut when fishing in a river for large fish in heavy water, and of lighter trout gut in the clear still water of a lake, or in a small stream: and as I invariably make the spoon take the place of the fly, attaching it to the upper portion of the casting line which I have already described, there is no need to give the swivel trace more than three strands of gut. I sketch below the arrangement of the spoon, flight, and trace complete.

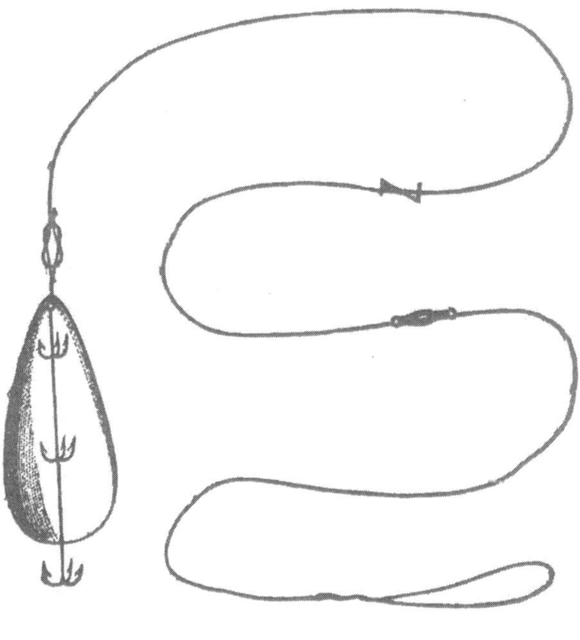

In use the fly-spoon should be thrown exactly like a large fly, and the cast should be invariably made at right angles to the shore-line, or to the line of the weeds, dropping the spoon as close to the edge as possible, and raising the point of the rod the instant that the spoon touches the water, so as to tempt the fish by its movement as soon as he is attracted by its splash in the water.

In one or two of the Kumaun lakes there are, as I shall presently describe, at certain seasons of the year, wide stretches of weed-encumbered shallow water, having here and there open spaces in which the mahsir delight to hunt the minnows. If the angler is tempted to try conclusions with the fish in those ticklish places, the spoon and the flight of hooks must be altered. It would be simply courting disaster to use a flight of three triplets, which must in an instant be hung up on the weeds. Under those circumstances I use a very small, almost circular, deeply bellied spoon having one eyed-triplet lying snug in its hollow. If a fish take this lure, the chances are that the triplet is well hidden in his mouth, and the angler is as free from the mischance of a hang-up in the weeds as if he had the fish on a single fly-hook.

I give a sketch below of the spoon and hooks, full size.

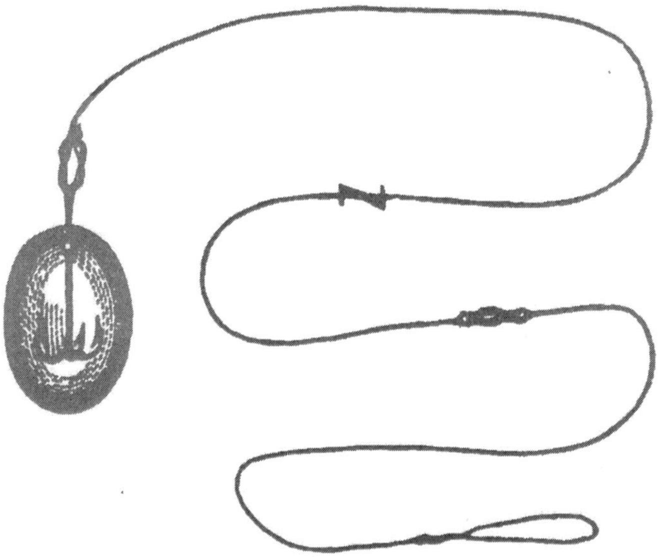

Having described and figured the fly-spoon as I have used it for many years, I must at the same time repeat that in the Kumaun lakes, as a rule, it is not a successful lure ; it is far inferior to the fly and ought only to be used as a last resource. With it, however, the biggest fish may, *on occasions*, be caught.

While indulging in this digression, I have left the angler slowly fishing round the Naini lake, while the shadow of Ayar-patha has been lengthening, and has finally touched the weir at the east-end of the lake. As a reward for his patience,

I here present him with an outline ground plan and section of the lake, copied from Mr. Ball's paper on the Kumaun lakes, and published in Volume XI of the Records of the Geological Survey of India. The scale of the plan is six inches to the mile; and the figures on the lake indicate the depth in fathoms. The figures in the section explain themselves.

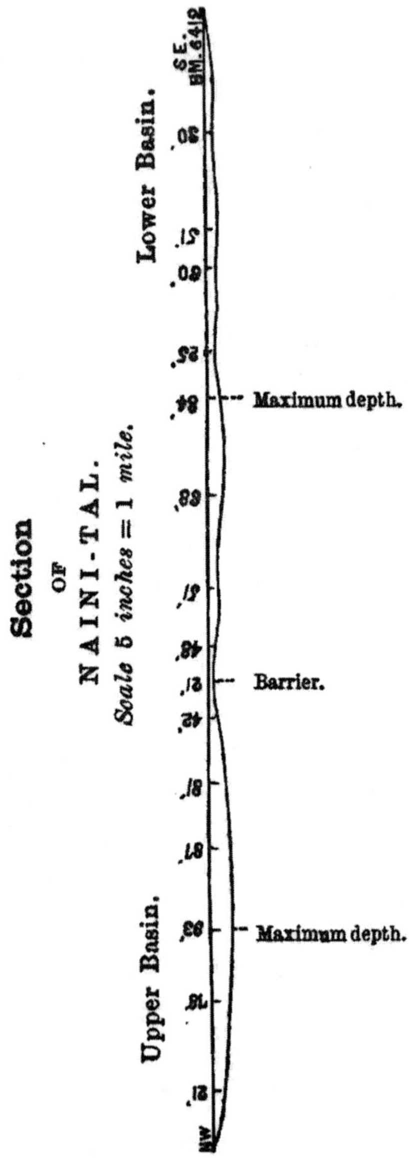

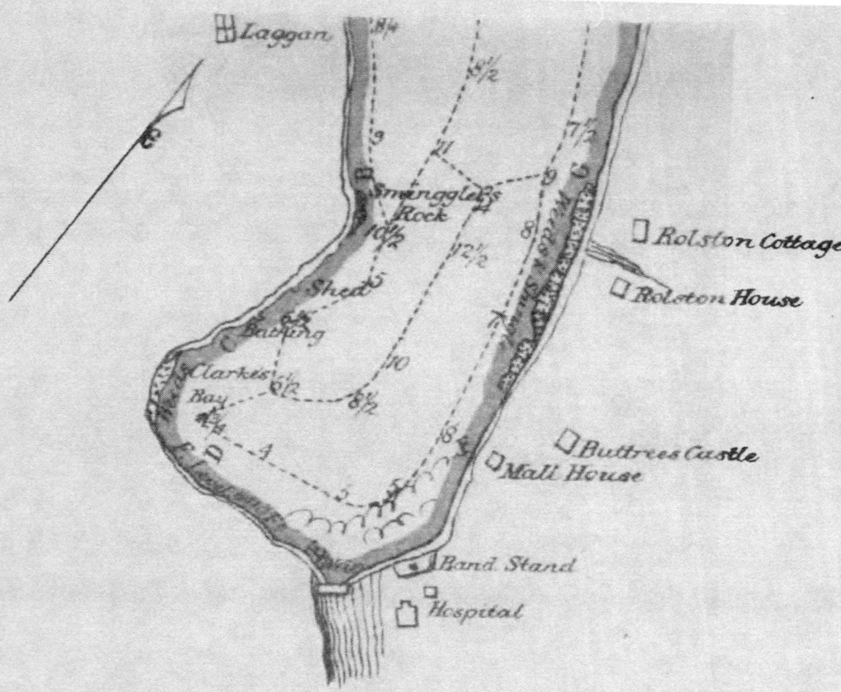

Soundings taken in 1871 by Dr. Amesbury.

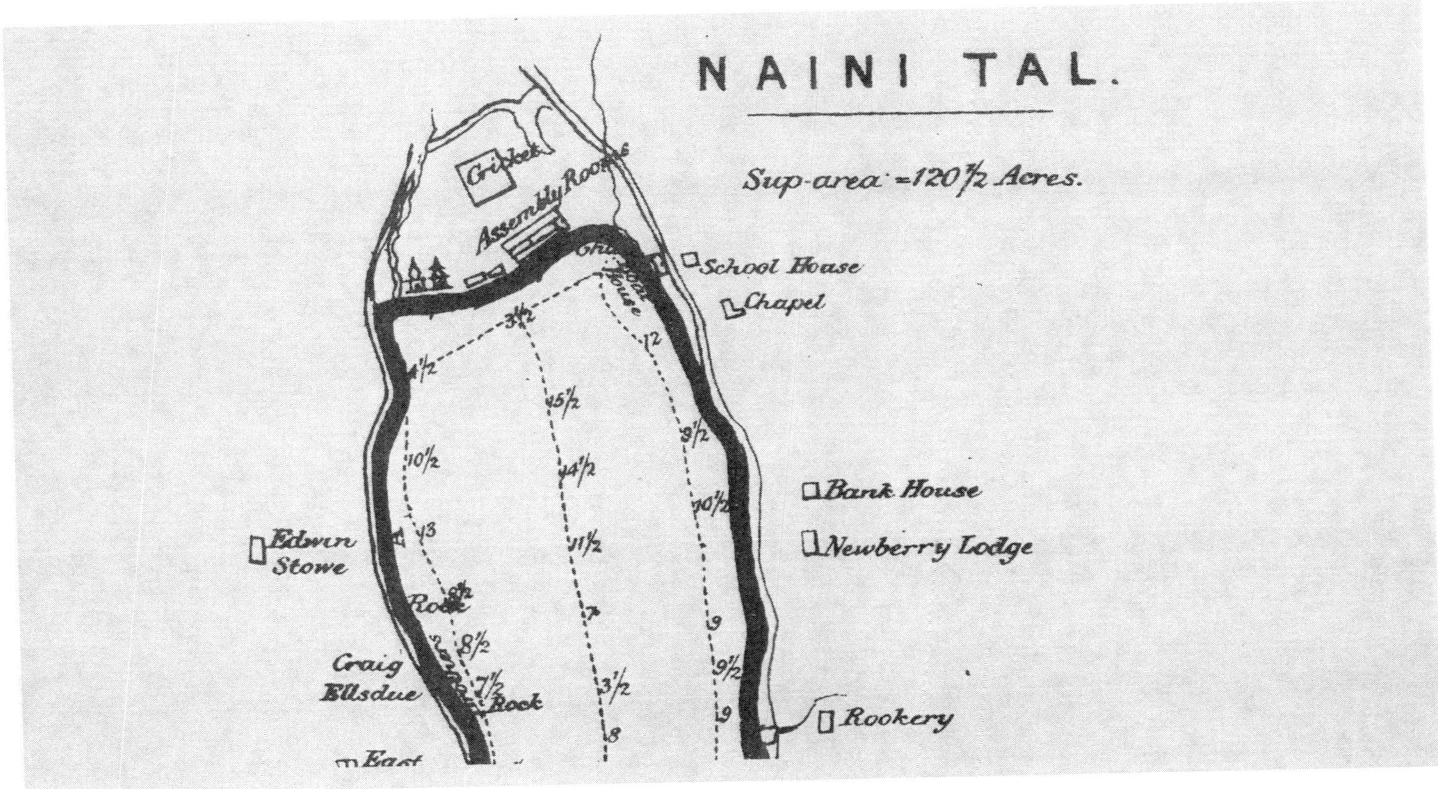
NAINI TAL.
Sup-area =120½ Acres.
Cricket
Assembly Rooms
School House
Chapel
Bank House
Newberry Lodge
Edwin Stowe
Rock
Craig Ellsdue
Rock
Rookery
East

Mahsir are to be caught all round the margin of the lake, but there are certain localities which, from having a deeper fringe of weeds affording more cover and a better supply of food, are more frequented by the fish than others. Among these I may note the stretch of shore from the level of Edwinstowe to the 'Smuggler's Rock.' (A to B on the plan.) One very favorite hold for big fish is in front of two huge masses of rock (named by me 'the brothers'), which lie half hidden in the water under the steep cliff of Craig-Ellachie that almost overhangs the lake where they lie. Here the fish are constantly on the feed; and in this corner I have secured many a heavy mahsir; while I am not ashamed to confess that I have lost many a good one, and had often to lament that I could not, alas! "get my twa and saxpenny hook out o' his mou."

If you have followed my advice and crept quietly up to within casting distance of 'the brothers,' and have dropped your fly like a falling poplar seed on the outer fringe of the weeds, you will mark as you raise the point of your rod the wake of a fish as he rushes after it from his hold; or you will perchance catch the gleam of a golden belly as the fish turns to seek the deeps, happily with your yellow spider firmly fixed in his mouth. Checked by the raising of the point of your rod, the fish may turn at once and come towards your boat, or he may rush onwards deep into the bed of weeds. In either case the business of your boatman is to pull the boat, for dear life, away from the weeds, and you on your part must risk your tackle by raising and even throwing well back the point of your rod, checking the run of the line as much as you dare. If you can keep the fish's head towards you, and can lift him even diagonally through the weeds into deep water, he is yours; but if he succeeds by his mad rush in embedding himself in the close set forest of weeds, and then turns, the chances against your landing him are ten to one. I have succeeded sometimes by judicious manœuvring and handling, by patience, by getting a passer-by on the shore to add terror to the position by pelting stones on the land side of the fish, and finally by reeling up short and using an oar to rake up weeds line and fish together! but, as a rule, you are doomed to lose your fish and more or less of your tackle.

One evening just opposite 'the brothers' I had a battle royal with a fish, which comes back vividly to my recollection. By his length and massiveness I judged him to be over twelve pounds in weight. When first checked by the hook he seemed to be struck all of a heap, and hesitated what to do: all the better for my chances of landing him,

I thought, as my boatman was getting judiciously away from the weeds; but his inaction did not last long. Up he came to the surface and shook the fly in his mouth as a terrier shakes a rat. Finding that I still had hold of him, he sank back and then with a rush sprang to his full length out of the water, his golden belly gleaming in the evening light: still he failed to gain his liberty, and at last bethought himself of his home in the weeds, and with the speed of an arrow, expended his last reserve of strength in a straight rush for his hold. I was forced to give him line, and when he turned he was locked fast so deep amongst the tangled weed stems that I had to break my cast to get rid of him.

Towards nightfall and in the grey dawn, I have often found the fish much less chary of leaving the weeds, allowing themselves to be led, I might say following the fly boldly out into deep water, showing fight only when too late. Not unfrequently under these circumstances, I have known a fish to pass under the boat in his hurry to follow the impulse given him when struck, and thus endanger the line by rasping it on the keel. As a rule, however, a fish when hooked will make for the weeds, and the skill of the angler will show itself in the nice discrimination of the amount of force which can be used without endangering his tackle, in the effort to compel the fish to make his first vigorous rush *parallel* to the weeds, and not into the thick of them.

On rare occasions, perhaps once or twice in a season, I have found the mahsir resorting in shoals to the base of the 'Smuggler's Rock.' My boatman would have it that the fish were in quest of a fly which at those times dropped from the bushes growing on the face of the rock. I never saw this fly, so I am unable to confirm or refute his supposition: but I am more inclined to think, from their peculiar movements, that the congregation of the fish was connected with some spawning ceremony; although the water at that point is 10 to 14 fathoms deep. Be the cause what it may, the appearance of a scuffle and turmoil at the base of the rock, and the sound of flapping on the water, should draw the fly-fisher with muffled oar to the spot. At such times I have landed four good fish in succession before the shoal got alarmed, and I have three times lost very large fish under identical circumstances. These fish were all too heavy to check in their downward rush; they each ran out many yards of line, plunging downwards like harpooned whales, then the casting line was felt to rasp on a ledge of rock, and the rod sprang straight. I have little doubt that at the base of the 'Smuggler's Rock' there is an overhanging ledge, under which the big fish dream away their days and nights, and to which they flee for shelter in their difficulties.

Passing eastward from the 'Smuggler's Rock' there are not many good casts, until the second soldier's bathing shed is passed. From thence round the whole of 'Clarke's Bay,' that is from C to D on the plan, the water should be fished carefully. This bay contains a very deep bank of weeds, and in it live some of the largest fish in the lake; but from its position and configuration it is not often that a satisfactory breeze can be got to curl the water on the weed line.

From 'Clarke's Bay' to the weir, through which the flood water of the lake passes, there are only one or two spots in which heavy fish live; the fringe of weeds is narrow, and the roadway passes close to the margin of the water. But it is along this shore that some of the best pitches for ground-bait fishing are to be found.

From the weir to the 'Mall House,' that is from E to F on the plan, passing in front of the Hospital and the old Band-stand, some of the best fishing on the lake is to be had; and before the angler can reach this point of his circuit, the shadows will have fallen on the lake, and the breeze from off China will most likely be flinging a lively ripple of wavelets on the edge of the bank of weeds. Fish carefully then, and you are bound tó have such sport as will make your blood tingle. It may not end in filling your basket, but it will certainly result in making you respect the prowess of the lake Mahsir; and if you have 'fishing in your bones' and love a bold and honest struggle, will make you long to fight the battle with them o'er again.

In this spot sacred to the very best fly-fishing on the lake (I am ashamed to tell the tale), the fish have during the past two seasons been harried by an unworthy pot-hunter armed with a 'demon prong.' Day after day the basking fish were subjected to this cruel persecution which had not even the merit of success. I myself saw floating decomposed and torn by this poacher's spear, two large fish; how many were scared, and what injury was done to legitimate sport, only those can say who can compare sport on the Naini lake now with what it was a few years ago.

Passing westwards up the lake, the whole of the water is worthy of careful fishing; but the most favourite haunts of the largest fish are from opposite 'Mall House' to 'Rolston Cottage' (F to G), and from the 'Rookery' on to the site of the 'Albion Hotel.' Just under 'Newberry Lodge,' one evening in the dusk, I hooked and landed after half-an-hour's play, a 16-lb. fish. In the dusk this fish did not see the boat, and so came sullenly but peaceably out into the deep water. I then reeled him up, and as he came within a few yards of the boat, he realized the situation, but alas! it was too late to struggle. I wore him down gradually, but at the very close of the battle, lost my landing net and very nearly lost the fish. My boatman, when raising the net to bag the fish, got him across the mouth of the net, instead of head foremost into it:—and in the sudden struggle that followed the touch of the metal, he lost his hold of the landing net and fish and net disappeared. Luckily the fish was exhausted, and bringing him again slowly up to the side of the boat, the boatman redeemed his credit by deftly lifting the monster with his hands, and thus consoled me for the loss of my landing net.

While recommending evening fishing, I can promise excellent sport to him who has the moral courage to be on the lake at half-past three o'clock on any warm still morning in summer. Many a time in years that are fled, I have wended my way down the hill, lantern in hand, feeling sure that my self-denial would be rewarded by my having the lake in solitude. Pushing off silently from the moorings, the faintest streak of dawn would be gleaming over Sher-ka-Danda, while the lake still lay in deep gloom. At casting distance the outline of the weed fringe cannot be made out, but never mind—drop your fly as near to the border line as you can, and draw it slowly and steadily towards you. At that time of the morning the fish will follow the fly for a long distance, and finally suck it down at the last moment; so be in no hurry to make your second cast. In perfect silence, like a spectre boat, move slowly on casting the fly over every yard of the water: only stopping at intervals to watch with wonder the sudden flashes of light which usher in morning over the Eastern hills and to listen to the wild call of the 'Kokla,' or the rich notes of the Black-bird or the clear tones of the Muezzin as he calls the Faithful to prayer from the mosque at the head of the lake. Each flash of light will bring the fringe of weeds more clearly into view; make the most of your time then, for so soon as it is broad day on the water your skill will be expended in vain, unless an early breeze spring up. On such occasions I have rarely remained on the lake after 6 o'clock: but I have frequently carried back with me, as the reward of my early rising, three fish weighing each from 5 lbs. to 7 lbs.: and sweeter still, I have freshened my day's work with

"Dreams of immortal morn, eternal May,
Old life, old sport of Lea-side and of Dove,
The life we cherish, and the sport we love."

On some of these early mornings it has been my lot to pass silently in front of the old Assembly-rooms while the drowsy band was still struggling to keep alive the spent energies of tired revellers, and grey dawn blurred the lights which had shone through the long night on the beauty and the chivalry of Naini-tal. Don't imagine, brother angler, that I made hard reflections on amusements which you and I perchance never had the capacity to enjoy; quite the contrary. I blessed the dear boys and girls in their young life's sport; examined with curious eye the faded elders still struggling to hold their places on the stage; sad pictures some of them at that hour of jaded and exhausted humanity, and passed on to my fishing with a heightened perception of the contrasts in life, as the last notes of the anthem mingled with the clear voice of the crier from the mosque, calling the Faithful to grateful thanksgiving for a comfortable night's rest in bed.

Some one will doubtless ask what is the outcome of Naini-tal fishing? and I must conscientiously reply that although the mahsir are more numerous in the lake than ever, the sport is poor and surrounded with difficulties. When I first angled in Naini lake, in 1863 and 1864, there were comparatively few large mahsir in it; there were shoals of the lake fish (Barbus Chilinoides) and many small trout (Barilius Bola). A morning's catch would include a couple of small mahsir, eight or nine 'lake-fish' and two or three trout. Gradually the mahsir have reduced the numbers of the other fish until it is a rare circumstance to catch a lake-fish with the fly, and I have not for many years seen a single trout, although I heard of one being caught last year by a troller.

In the year 1875 I was living at Naini-tal 'en garçon,' and having no dread of the penalties that awaited Tam O'Shanter when he kept late hours, I fished on many warm evenings till 9 or 9-30 P.M. I kept a record of my captures during that season from the 15th April till the 20th July when I left the valley on leave. In those three months I bagged over 250 lbs. weight of mashir, fishing on four evenings each week and occasionally in the early morning. Alas! these Halcyon days are gone. I can still recommend any angler who can throw a fly successfully on such streams as the Itchin, to try his hand on the mahsir of the Naini lake at any season of the year; but really good sport can be had only early in the year, before the season has begun, while yet the barges, and the depot whale boats, and the club racers, and the loving canoes are lying slime covered in their winter docks.

At all seasons, however, there is legitimate sport

to be had in ground-bait fishing or in fishing with a live minnow. The Municipality exacts a License-tax of two rupees per month from each rod, and yet a number of natives make a livelihood out of the ground-bait fishing; and on occasions I have seen fish weighing 20 to 25 lbs. landed by these fishermen. They find a ready sale for whatever they can catch at eight annas per pound, a price at which one can buy tinned California Salmon in the shops. I have often explained to these men the construction and use of the ledger tackle, with which I have no doubt greater success might be attained, but they are too conservative and obstinately adhere to the ordinary line and float, which to the highly educated Naini fish is an object of derision. In vain is the net spread in the sight of any bird, and equally in vain is a lump of the most nutty flavored paste laid in front of a mahsir if he sees a strong piece of gut leading straight from it to a float between him and the sky.

I have written only of the mashir in the Naini lake, because they now reign supreme, having practically, as far as fly-fishing is concerned, cleared out every other kind of fish. The instinct of the trout, which led it in autumn to crowd round the mouth of the stream which enters the lake at its western end, accelerated its disappearance :

for I have in former years often seen the natives lifting them out with sheets in hundreds as they pressed on each other in their anxiety to get up stream. The persistence with which this instinct remained in the Baril is in strange contrast to the complete annihilation of the migratory tendency in the lake Mahsir. In a long series of years I have only once heard of a mahsir being caught five hundred yards up the main stream which feeds the lake. Even in the first heavy freshets in the beginning of the rains, they never make any attempt to pass up the stream, but are content to enjoy their bath of fresh water on the surface of the lake.

The spawning grounds of the mahsir are little quiet gravelly nooks, inside the fringe of weeds, a fact of which the native poacher is well aware, as it enables him now and again to snatch a few fish with a leaded triplet, which he drives mercilessly into the belly of the unwary spawner as she rolls and rubs herself along the gravelly bottom.

Dr. Day has remarked, and I can confirm his observation, that the mahsir when spawning scarcely, if at all, loses condition. The process occupies the fish at intervals for a couple of months or even longer; as the eggs ripen they are deposited, but there is no need to enforce a close season to protect the spawning fish; nor have I ever seen a mahsir in the evil condition of a lately spawned 'kelt.'

For the table there is no fish more "worthy of a grace, as long's your arm," than a 6-lb. lake mahsir *caught on the fly.* The difference between a fish caught with the fly and one of the same size caught by ground bait is Hyperion to a Satyr. The latter is always soft and muddy-tasted; while the former has firm, flaky, curdy flesh, with a nutty flavour. Boil him in salt water, my brother, and eat him with oyster sauce *when you can afford it*, and you will have a dish fit to share with the best of gentle and honest anglers.

CHAPTER III.

BHIM-TAL.

HAVING spent a week on the Naini lake, and drank your fill of the beauties of rock and water and shaggy wood, you will make an early start some morning for Bhim-tal. If I am to accompany you, your start must be an early one. Let the gongs in the lower Bazaar strike six on your ear, as you pass out of the shady valley, and are suddenly bathed in the flood of sunlight breaking over the Nepal hills. There is no more lovely ride in the Kumaun hills than the sinuous path which you will follow round the slopes of Sher-ka-Danda and Lyriakanta, now dipping into a deep gully with its brawling torrent, now lingering in the shade of the oaks and rhododendra, and anon basking in the glorious sunlight as the road glides over the steep grassy slopes of the Eastern spurs of Lyriakanta—all the while you may feast on a glorious view of the Sub-Himalayan Forest and Terai stretched at your feet—wide patches of lovely green fields encroaching on the primæval forest, a monument to the wisdom and energy of the best man that ever swayed the sceptre in Kumaun.

Arrived at the sloping shoulder of the mountain, the road turns downwards to the Bhowali stream, passing Bhowali House about the fifth mile. For about a quarter of a mile after passing the water mill and bunnia's shop the path keeps the right bank of the little stream, and as you watch the water curling under the banks, brawling over the shallows and eddying round the rocks, your heart will jump to its music, for it recalls the days long fled, when you followed the windings of the burn down the heath covered hill, and through the sweet smelling birch woods—and filled your basket with the speckled trout. The burn is there and the overshadowing trees, and the sweet glints of sunshine sparkling on the water, but the merry trout live only in the exile's dreams :

> " Dreams of accustomed fields and haunts of yore,
> " Trout dimpled pool, and babbling brook and burn."

Crossing the stream, the road, after an ascent of about a hundred yards, reaches the lowest point of the long ridge which forms the Northern or

North-Western boundary of the Bhim-tal valley and begins at once a rapid descent. I know of no lovelier view than that which is spread below the traveller as he crosses this ridge. The narrow valley stretches away before him in descending terraces, bounded on the North and South by two high wood-covered ranges; in the near distance the lake of Bhim-tal glistens in the sunlight, and the white bungalow throws out a signal of welcome, while farther off and apparently, though not really, on a higher level a glimpse is obtained of Naukuchia Lake, nestling under its low rounded hills, backed by some loftier mountains, one of which a sugar-loaf peak is singularly prominent and striking.

The distance by road from Naini-tal to Bhim-tal is eleven miles, but it actually lies only six miles, as the crow flies, to the East South-East of Naini-tal. From Katgodam Railway Station by the direct road the lake is nine miles distant. Its elevation above the sea-level is about 4,500 feet; so that the difference in level between Naini-tal and Bhim-tal is about 1,900 feet. The maximum length of the lake is 5,580 feet, and its greatest width 1,490 feet, while nowhere has it a greater depth than 87 feet at flood-level. There is, however, a very great difference between the low water and flood level. The difference between the

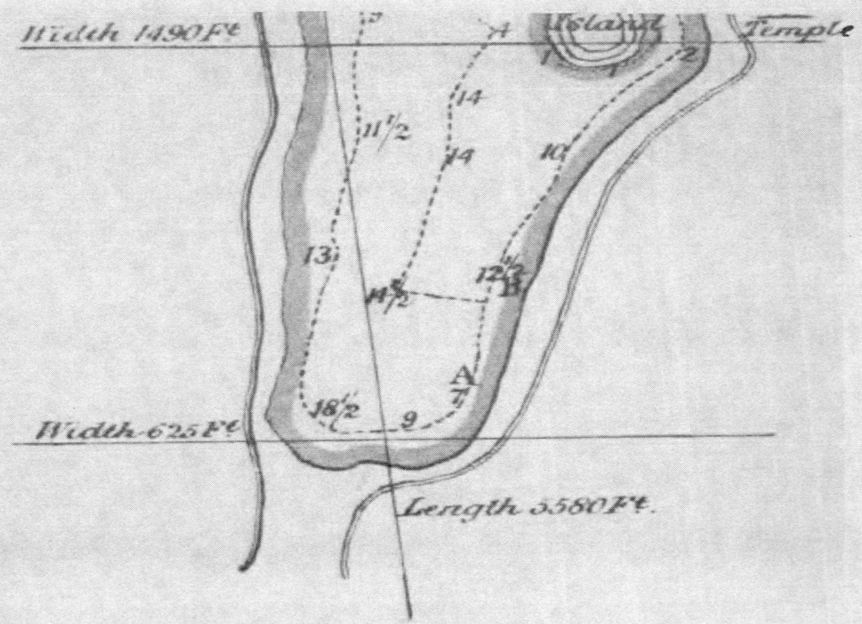

Soundings taken in 1871 by Dr. Amesbury.

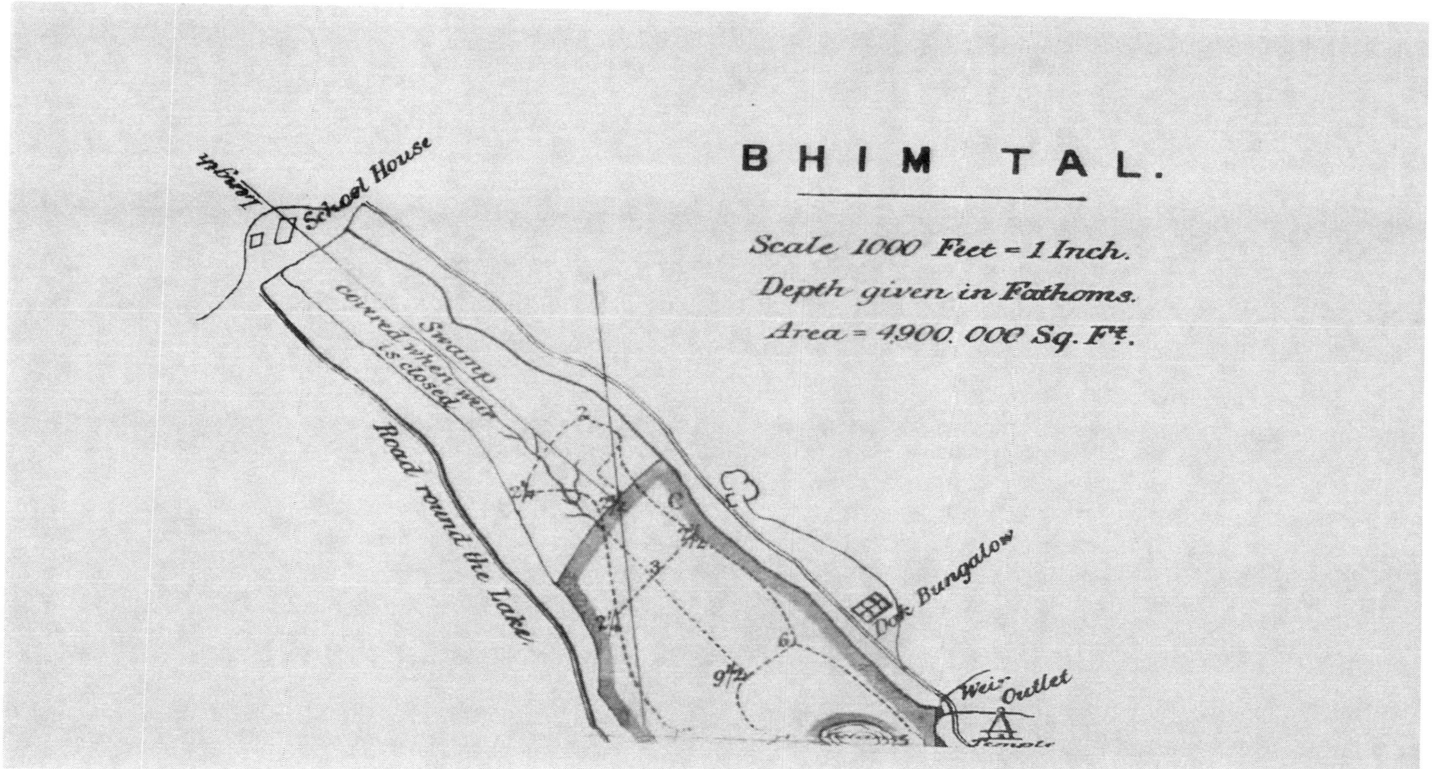

BHIM TAL.
Scale 1000 Feet = 1 Inch.
Depth given in Fathoms.
Area = 4,900. 000 Sq. Ft.
School House
Length
Swamp
covered when weir
is closed
Road round the Lake.
Dak Bungalow
Weir
Outlet

level of the flooring of the bund and the escape is 36 feet, and usually about 10 feet of the escape gap is closed, so that the water in the lake rises 46 feet during the rainy season, and falls to the same extent during March and April.

The general direction of the length of the lake is from North-West to South-East, and the position of the embankment and escape is about half-way round the Eastern side. Overlooking the embankment stands the Dâk Bungalow.

The existing weir is the second which has been constructed within the past ten years. The first embankment brought the old temple and its overshadowing elm trees within the grasp of the lake: the trees perished, and the impiety of the authorities in flooding the Temple and keeping the feet of the Mahadeo wet for so many months every year was, according to an old *Jogi*, justly punished by the demolition of the structure in the floods of 1880. The new weir has been built so as to exclude the temple; and I was told by the same high ecclesiastical authority, that due respect having been paid to the feelings of the presiding deity the embankment would now stand for many years.

From an angler's point of view, I am afraid that I cannot wish the weir a long life. The rise and fall of the water in the lake is so great that the fish never seem to settle into holds, but wander about aimlessly, so that success in hitting them off must depend very much on knowledge of their habits and of the food-supply available for them under changing circumstances.

In April the whole of the surplus water is sent down the Gola river to replenish the Bhabar canals, and as a consequence Bhim-tal, until the rains fall and the waters are again shut up, presents anything but a picturesque appearance. Half of the valley is dry and covered with grass and sedge, while the deeper portions of the lake have an ugly border of steep shingly bank, between the margin of the water and the fringe of bushes and grass which marks the high water line. A picturesque scrub-covered island which stands in front of the weir when the lake is full, disappears as the water escapes; and altogether Bhim-tal loses much of its beauty till the month of August when it is again filled up.

As regards accommodation to be had there is the Dâk Bungalow available under the usual restrictions of tenure of occupancy; but it may be mentioned that, as it is much frequented by travellers to Almora and Ranikhet, &c., the authorities discourage loungers and all the angling brotherhood by doubling the rate of hire after the first 48 hours.

Luckily within the past two years the accommodation at the lake has been supplemented by the erection of a large double storied building on the West side, and by a small chalet on the banks of the lake. These buildings are due to the enterprise of Mr. Jones, Proprietor of the Bhim-tal Tea Gardens, to whom application may be made for permission to occupy them. The buildings may be hired in suites of rooms, and they are fairly and usefully furnished, cooking vessels, crockery, glass, &c., being supplied. The rents vary from Rs. 30 per month for one suite of rooms to Rs. 60 or Rs. 70 for more extensive accommodation.

Several boats are on the lake for hire at the rate of one rupee per day.

Having made a "good, honest, wholesome hungry breakfast," at the pleasure of your host, the Dâk Bungalow Khansamah, put up your rod and get your tackle in order; lay a fine trout casting line in water to be thoroughly soaked, and take your ease in contemplation or in the company of a congenial book, until the sun has turned towards the west. The middle of the day is good only for bottom fishing.

When the lake is full, there are few lovelier scenes than that on which the eye rests looking up the valley from the verandah of the Dâk

Bungalow. The waters of the lake at its western end rest against a low round hillock, on which are a few trees and the village school-house; behind lie the terraced tea gardens and the sloping braes which lead the eye up to the forest-clad spurs of Sher-ka-Danda; while, above all, in the blue hazy distance towers the summit of China. Therefore it is no hardship to condemn you for a few hours to restful enjoyment of the scene.

The range which bounds the valley to the south and west gives early cover to the retreating sun, and as soon as you note that the shadows are deepening on the south side of the lake, get your tackle together, and pull gently over to the south-west corner. At this point the stream which collects the water from the upper part of the valley flows into the lake. Its own channel is deeply cut and tortuous, but where it debouches into the lake, there are flats and shallows on which the larger mahsir delight to hunt the minnows of an afternoon, and there you should begin to test your skill. You may pass up the stream in your boat for some distance, but the channel is too narrow and the water too clear to admit of progress undiscovered by the fish. In the rainy season when the stream is pouring a volume of muddy water into the lake, I have seen a brother angler make a good bag of lake fish here, using the worm and float; but in clear weather and in clear water no success can be anticipated except by means of the fly or the fly-spoon.

Having made a few casts over the shallows near the mouth of the stream, you should pass slowly along the southern shore, which will be completely in shadow, using one or other of the four flies I have described in connexion with Naini-tal, and occasionally trying a cast with a small fly-spoon. Fair-sized fish will rise all along the southern bank, when the water is low; and you will at once note the difference of the habitat forced on the fish by the circumstances of the locality. In Naini-tal, where there is no great difference between low water and flood-level, the weed fringe is permanent, and the fish have their homes amongst them. In Bhim-tal, except at the shallow western end, there are no weeds, and the fish rest where they can amongst the rough angular pieces of quartz and shale that form the steep sides of the lake bed. Often they will be found lying close to the edge of the water; and, as a rule, it is best to drop the fly almost on the stones, drawing it slowly away towards the deeper water. Most frequently when the fly has got about a yard distant from the shore, the swirl of a fish from below, or the gleam of his golden belly as he turns will be seen; but not seldom a fish will spring out from the loose stones at the very edge of the water. Mahsir generally take the fly under the water, seizing it as they sweep past in a wild rush, but very rarely making a second attempt. The lake-fish, on the other hand, frequently spring out of the water in their eagerness to take the fly, and they generally show some portion of their bodies above water in their rise; but like the mahsir they very seldom make a second rush in real earnest. This is very different from the barils, which will make one attempt after another to take the fly, and die rather than that their prey should escape.

There being no weeds in the greater part of Bhim-tal, the hair-breadth escapes in playing a fish and the many losses of tackle are absent. Get a fish once well hooked and in the act of running out a taut line, and with ordinary care you may regard him as bagged. For the same reason it is not absolutely necessary to limit your cast to one fly; you may with safety add a drop fly; but for my own part I never use one.

When you have reached the east end of the lake, make your boatman rest on his oars until the eastern shore is darkened by the shadow of the opposite hill. If you are one who, as I suppose, makes contemplation the complement of his sport, let the flood of evening light gilding the sides and summit of the hill above Sangri sink into your memory against the day when "those that look out of the windows shall be darkened," and drink in the sweet sounds that float over the water against the hour when "the daughters of music shall be brought low." Listen to the tinkle of the bells as the cattle wend their homeward way; the bark of the 'Khaker,' startled while grazing on the slope of the hill; the wild scream of the fish hawk as she changes her perch on the dead stumps of overhanging trees; and the friendly chatter of the babblers as they hurry home through the bushes. You will thus be able to return to your office table, and to the unsavoury court-house, in the dust and heat of the plains, with a wealth of sweet memories that will stand you in better stead than the prescriptions of your doctor. You may see him now as he drives down the mall in his buggy, severely totalling up your symptoms, and worrying himself with thoughts of the return of that groaning hypochondriac whom he has got rid of for a few weeks. But he will fail to recognize you as you hop out of the train, the "honesty of the open air" on your cheek and fire in your eye consigning all his prescriptions to a region even hotter than the station platform.

As evening closes fish slowly back along the eastern and northern margins of the lake. The best fish will be found at a point (A—B), where the bank has slipped from the road above, about three hundred yards from the east end of the lake. You may, however, fish hopefully every yard of the water until the cold west wind begins to blow down the valley from the heights of the Ghagur Range. Then the fish will cease to rise, and it is useless to weary yourself in vain efforts to tempt them.

There is one exception to this rule. Occasionally in very hot weather the Dadu does not begin to blow until very late. On those occasions the fish will keep on the rise, and if you care for night-fishing, take off your light gut cast, attach your fly to the strongest trout gut you may have on your casting line, and fish boldly. These are the occasions which justify men in stating that mahsir will take any fly offered to them:—that he is a fish with no discrimination and will prefer the fringe of a bath towel to the most scientifically tied fly out of Farlow's shop. With this view I cannot agree, and I shall give my reasons further on; but I admit the fact that on rare and special occasions, in the hot weather, and especially at night, the fish rise so keenly that they will take any fly presented to them;

and the veriest tyro at fly-fishing will bring home three or four good fish. Ordinarily, however, as much care, as much silence and absolute quiet are necessary for night-fishing as during the day. A well trained boatman will make your boat glide noiselessly within a few yards of the bank or of the bushes, and will stop her dead at the sound of a flop in the water as a fish rises. With a quick glance upwards to make sure of overhanging boughs, switch your fly well in towards the bank, and draw it slowly towards you; the feeding fish will take the fly at once, and be utterly astonished to find that he is checked in his attempt to wheel back under the bushes to his favourite swim. The boatman pulls sharply out while the fish struggles in a vain attempt to shake off the 'painter';—and at last comes sulkily out, following the lead of the taut line. You will have no trouble with him until you reel him into close proximity to the boat, when he will make his first rush to a distance and with a dash that will astonish you, and make you thank your stars that you had secured a good 'offing' and sea-room.

Not a few of the pink-eyed lake-fish are still to be caught in Bhim-tal, but their numbers have fallen off sadly of late years. I have notes of two days' fishing in Bhim-tal, which I enjoyed in

June 1873 just before the monsoon broke. I fished with the finest trout tackle, and a cast of three small trout flies, a grey midge, a black gnat and a red spider, and spending three hours morning and evening on the lake, I came home on each occasion with over three dozen fish. In those days there were no mahsir in Bhim-tal, and the lake-fish rarely ran over a pound in weight; but there were many of them, and with fine tackle they gave excellent sport.

Without doubt the mahsir have lessened the numbers of the lake-fish; but there is as little doubt that the protection of the fish from poachers is too intermittent to secure the interests of the honest angler. Of late years, Mr. Docherty, the supervisor of the irrigation works, has done all in his power to put down poaching; but during the rains the lake-fish follow their migratory instincts and pass up the main feeder in large shoals into a shallow pond which lies close under the Bhim-tal tea gardens. In that pond I have known the villagers from Mahrgaon hold a nocturnal revel with torches and nets and carry off maunds of spawning fish. All along the course of the stream flowing into the lake the fish have to run the gauntlet from many enemies. On the margin of the lake I have again and again found the pounded leaves and milky juice of a species of

Bauhinia, which is used largely to stupefy and poison fish, and I have seen many dead fish floating in the weeds out of reach of the poisoner. A pair of fish-hawks are always at work on the lake, but they are 'honest anglers.' Otters I have never seen, nor have I ever found traces of them in this lake nor in Naini-tal. I was once assured by a pair of young anglers that they had not only seen but fired some shots from an express rifle at a couple of otters. Dear boys! for once in their lives they may congratulate themselves on their bad shooting, for I ascertained from the khansama of the dâk bungalow, that the youngsters had mistaken the heads of two buffaloes enjoying an afternoon swim for wily otters, and did their very best to bag them.

Morning fishing in Bhim-tal is not in my experience so successful as in some of the other lakes. The reason of this is to be sought in the persistence of the cold night wind, which continues to blow down the valley till 9 o'clock, or even later. When the sun is well up, however, it is time to be stirring. Get into your boat and fish down the lake on the eastern side, drifting with the breeze and dropping your fly into the shadows of the high bank. If the weir is closed, and the lake well filled, a few good fish will be found round the island and between the island and the weir. Fishing slowly and carefully you will be aware that before you have reached the east end of the lake, the west wind has gradually fallen, and quite at the end of the lake it will be a dead calm. Let the boatman rest on his oars, for it is worse than useless to attempt fishing up the west side of the lake in a dead calm, and having the morning sun behind you. Wait patiently till the eastern breeze begins to blow up the lake in gentle gusts; you need never weary of the sights and sounds that claim your wondering notice. The morning has ushered in a new day, and with it have started into active life a thousand objects claiming your loving admiration. The restless swoop and glitter of a hundred dragon flies as they hunt their prey, quenching their fiery colors in the lake only to rouse them again in the fierce sunlight; the hum of a thousand bees as they gather sweets from the catkins of the willow; the morning call of the black partridge to his mate; the anxious human-like bustle of the lap-wing amongst the stones by the lake's edge, striving in vain to make her callow young lie still under the cover of the rocks; the sinuous track of a water-snake on the search for frogs; the cuckoo and the mag-pie and the bul-bul, all will strive to win your attention from the glorious sunlight gilding the ragged woods and serrated hill-tops, and flashing along the water, now at length sparkling like a million diamonds in the fresh eastern breeze.

If the date of your visit be shortly after the closing of the weir, when the rising waters of the lake are beginning to overflow the flat land at its upper end which has lain dry and covered with grass and sedge for some months, you are pretty certain of good sport. The fish seek those shallows on account of the insect food so plentiful on them, and with an easterly breeze sharply curling the water you cannot fail to lure a fish or two to your fly. Should you hook a fish, hold him as hard as you dare, else he will give you much trouble by circling round the sedge and weed stalks.

On your homeward journey by the west side of the lake and as you leave the weed-covered shallows, look out for a large tree growing on the steep bank, at a point (C) where, when the lake is low, a lovely spring of delicious water gushes out of the hill-side. This spring is covered as the water rises, and in its neighbourhood I have very often found bold and willing fish keeping their court, and have bagged not a few in this spot. They seem to be attracted partly by the fresh spring water, and partly by the remains of food of sorts which are, no doubt, left round the spring by the Paharis when cooking their food there.

In the stream which enters the head of the lake there is to be found a small species of Barilius which in the gravelly runs takes a small fly (black or grey) freely. The sport is little better than chilwa fishing, but neither is it to be despised. Many a pleasant evening half hour have I spent whipping for chilwas, and often have I added fresh white-bait to the menu of the camp dinner, when the lordly mahsir or dainty mullet was not to be had.

There is, I believe, good ground-bait fishing to be enjoyed from the weir and from the north-west bank of the lake; but I have no experience of it. For the past two years I have noticed a gang of three or four professional 'bankers' fishing here, sending their fish over-night to Nainital and selling them there as fresh caught Naini fish. These men rarely trouble themselves to sit near their rods. Fixing them firmly in a heap of stones, and placing a small pebble on the reel in such a position that the handle of the reel in its first revolution must receive a smart check when a fish carries off the bait, they thus ensure the fish being struck and hooked automatically. The fisherman returns at his leisure to inspect his rod, and land any fish that may be clamorous for his services.

Another form of fishing I have seen used very

successfully by the boys of the villages near. They bait a hook with a small black cricket which is found under the stones near the lake, and wading into the shallows rarely fail to catch a few lake-fish, more especially if their pitch has been well puddled by the village buffaloes before the sport began.

Bhim-tal is occasionally troubled by a development of an infusorial animalcule which discolors the water, and puts a considerable optical obstruction in the way of fly-fishing. I have seen the same development, but at intervals of some years, in the Naini lake and also in Malwa-tal and in Sath-tal; but I have never seen it in Naukuchia, the waters of which I have always found clear and pellucid, so that one can see the bottom at 10 to 15 feet. The creature concerned is microscopic, and I believe is one of the Peridineœ; it can be made out by the naked eye as a floating speck, and during its life seems to change color, from appearing, *in the mass*, of a greyish clay colour to a reddish brown. On occasions I have seen the whole body of water colored of one uniform greyish green tint; and a wag of my acquaintance nearly brought a duel on himself by comparing the fiery red head of a Scotch gunner, having his morning swim in Naini-tal, to a carrot floating in a bowl of pea-soup! Often these infusoria are developed unequally and appear in long wavy bands streaking the lake with color. They are closely allied to forms which are sometimes developed in the ocean in great numbers, imparting color to vast tracts of sea water. Similar species are also well known to frequent Alpine lakes in Europe, but only where the water is of great purity. My observations lead me to conclude that they have no effect on angling except in so far as they prevent the fish from seeing the fly or spoon at any great distance. Sport will still be good if the fish are hugging the shore, where the water is shallow. So that I would encourage the angler tò ply his craft even if the lake should be of a most unpromising color.

It occurs to me here to record what little I have to say on the kind of weather which is favourable or the reverse to Himalayan lake fly-fishing. After an experience of 24 years, I have made up my mind on two points only regarding angler's weather on these lakes, and both these points are negative. Firstly, you will never get a fish to rise to a fly while a thunder-storm is going on, even at a distance; nay, when the clouds are massed in that unmistakeable fashion which indicates disturbing electrical conditions, although no storm may be waking the echoes, fish will not rise to the fly. Secondly, when the clouds are actually resting on the lake, whether there is wind or not, the fish will refuse to move.

Apart from those two general conditions, I cannot say that I have determined any atmospherical states to be specially adverse or favourable to fly-fishing. During a long spell of fair weather with a high barometer, the feeding of the fish seems to me to depend more on the time of the day, and the quiet undisturbed state of the lake, than on any other circumstances.

Very often during heavy temporary showers unaccompanied by thunder and lightning I have had excellent sport. Again after a violent thunderstorm with heavy rain which has cleared the air and left behind the crispness of an October morning in England, I have had the very best of sport. And on three or four occasions on Naini-tal, preceding torrential rain with a very low barometer and a gale blowing from the east so strong that my boatman could with difficulty keep the boat to the wind, I have found the mahsir mad with excitement, seizing the fly or attempting to seize it on every cast. One of these memorable occasions was on the evening of the 16th September 1880. Next day 13·7 inches of rain fell, and on the 18th, 18·10 inches more, resulting in the great landslip which engulphed in its sudden swoop 43 Europeans and 143 natives.

My conclusion, therefore, is, that, barring the two general atmospherical conditions which I have named, one may fish with fair prospect of success in all weathers from March till the end of September on Naini-tal, and from March till the middle of October on the lower lakes.

CHAPTER IV.

NAUKUCHIA-TAL.

"Thou know'st it well—nor fen, nor sedge,
Pollute the pure lake's crystal edge."

NAUKUCHIA—the nine cornered-lake—lies as figured on the map about 1½ miles to the south-east of Bhim-tal. To any one who has shot chikor, and rested awhile on the slopes of the mountain above the villages of Sangri and Padani, the suggestion must at once have arisen that the whole valley from the terraces of the Bhim-tal tea gardens and the lands of Mahrgaon in the north-west, right up to the eastern boundary of Naukuchia-tal was at one time covered by a continuous sheet of water. The existing lakes of Bhim-tal and Naukuchia-tal are simply portions of this large lake, whose waters at that time found their way to the Gola river down the ravine leading from the southern corner of Bhim-tal. Standing under the old toon trees which shade the village of Padani, and looking across to the rugged gap in the continuous boundary line of the valley through which the waters of both lakes now reach the Gola, one must concede the highest probability to this suggestion. Mr. Theobald, in his paper on the Kumaun lakes (Records, Geological Survey, Vol. XIII, Part 3), has, while explaining his view of glacial action in the production of the lakes, fully admitted the probability of the former continuity of Bhim-tal and Naukuchia.

The latter is an irregularly shaped and most picturesque sheet of water. I have never been able to count up its nine corners, and perhaps it is as well that I never tried; for the Padan of Sirori assured me solemnly that any mortal who should see its nine corners *all at once* would perish miserably in its waters. There is a weird beauty about Naukuchia lake far surpassing any of the others. It lies snugly nestled against the bank which cuts the sky line to the south and which Mr. Theobald, on good grounds, regards as the moraine bed left by the retreating Mahrgaon glacier, and is surrounded by low wooded or scrub-covered hills. The pathway from Bhim-tal leads you on to a delicious gently sloping

NAUKUCHIA TAL.

Scale 1000 Feet = 1 Inch.

Depth given in fathoms.

Area = 4,849,500 Sq. Ft.

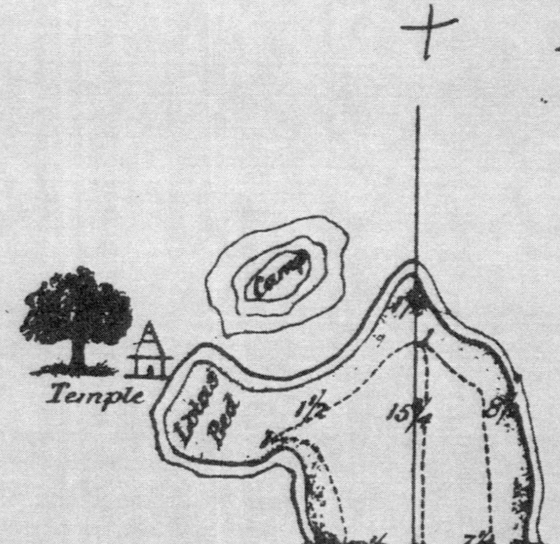

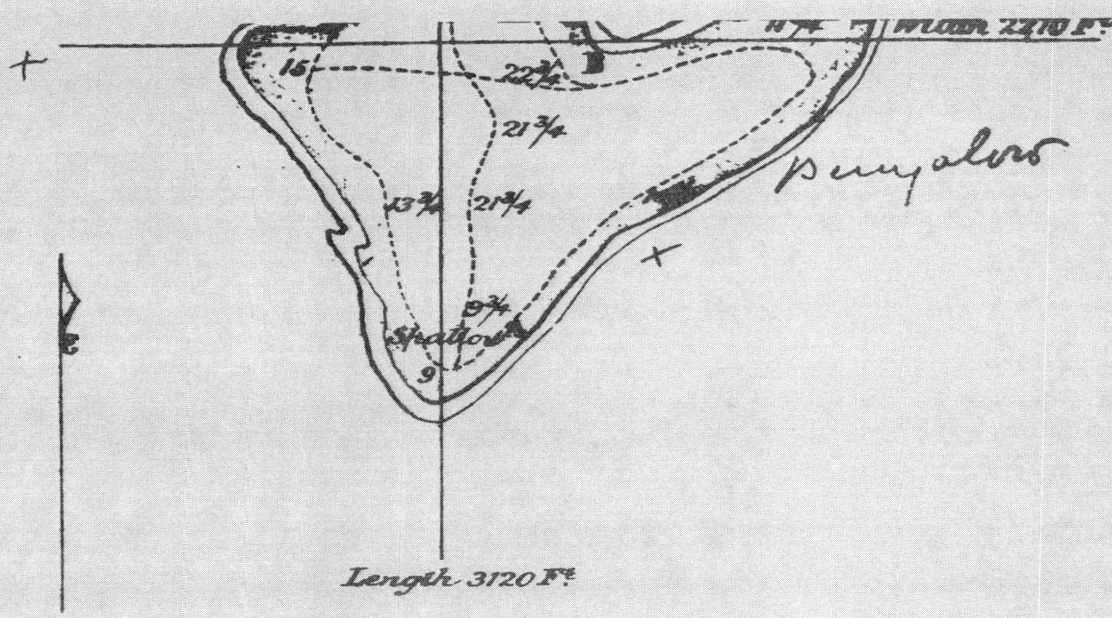

Soundings taken in 1871 by Dr. Amesbury.

heavily at Naukuchia, and your men must have cover if they are to escape fever.

"When the sun gangs wast the hill" you will, I hope, find yourself underweigh in your boat. There are good fish among the lotus plants at the north-west angle of the lake, but it is useless to tempt them as it would be impossible to land them. I have seen large mahsir feeding inside the lilies close under the old pipul-tree: Epicureans of the first guild industriously top-dressing their meal of silvery minnows with a dessert of green figs, as they dropt ripe from the old tree into their mouths. But you may as well pass on beyond the lotus-covered corner, fishing carefully along the west side of the lake.

You will at once perceive a vast difference between the banks of the Naukuchia lake and those of Bhim-tal. Here there is no weir to hold up the water, and there is so little difference between low and flood water-level, that the grass and shrubs growing on the edge of the lake never suffer from excess moisture. The cover for the fish is perfect; and if you can deftly land your fly under the overhanging boughs, using fine gut and a long cast, I will guarantee an answering challenge from a fish at every second or third throw. The crystal clearness of the water makes it an absolute essential to success that every cast be made with the utmost care and precision. Thick shrubs push themselves forward under overhanging trees, leaving narrow shadowy bays between. Search those bays carefully with your fly and you cannot fail to have sport if the fish are feeding. As you glide silently round you will see the fish rising at the edge of the bushes; coming from under the boughs to secure the insects that circle round the outer branches and dip and re-dip their worn-out wings in the water, as their short day of joysome life draws wearily to its close. There, a little to your left, rose a fine fish; let the boat move more in front of his hold, make a cast or two over the water you have just left, to steady your hand, there is no hurry, and you cannot afford to bungle the cast, as the fish will give you only one chance. Lift the line clean by the spring of your rod, and with your arm hand and rod all of one piece, bring the fly forward with that unexplainable twitch of your wrist which comes only to the experienced fly-fisher, and, as the fly drops with a midge like flight on the water, your fish will sweep out in a lordly fashion from beneath the boughs, followed, like all big men, by half-a-dozen toadies, and, as you raise the point of your rod, you will be surprised by the sound of a check-winch running out at fifty miles an hour, while your line comes home limp and slack, and your fish has disappeared. Turning round angrily to see who has mocked your misfortune, and throwing your eye round the margin of the lake in search of a brother angler, the sound will again strike your ear as the very best imitation of a fast-running check-winch you have ever heard; but you will at the same instant discover that the musician is only a small coot, diving and fluttering and skipping in amorous mood with some companions outside the lotus beds. Don't swear at him; for you have not yet let him hear the music of *your* winch, and he has no thoughts of mocking you:

> "He doth but sing, because he must,
> And pipes but as the linnets sing."

Your next cast will be more successful, and, as the shadows grow deeper and evening falls, the fish will become bolder. When you are nearing the east end of the lake the water shallows, and here, if in any spot, it is worth your while to try a small gold fly-spoon. On the 20th September 1886, I hooked, and had an exciting run from a very large mahsir in this corner of the lake; and the same evening off a point of land on the south side, I hooked, and landed after half-an-hour's fight, a fish which, after being cleaned and sent into Naini-tal, weighed 21 lbs.

I cannot say why it should be the case, but it is an unquestionable fact that the fish in the Naukuchia Lake are more keen to rise at the "Silver Doctor" than at any other fly I have ever offered to them. Mr. H. Ross first pointed out this predilection to me, and I soon had an opportunity of practically verifying it; for fishing on the lake in June 1885, when there were four rods on the water besides my own, several of them wielded by skilled hands, the fish refused to move in any numbers to any fly but the "Silver Doctor." I had some trouble in making up flies to supply my own wants and those of a brother angler in my company, but the results repaid the trouble; for I succeeded in landing 60 fish, the largest being 9 lbs., and my companion bagged 30 fish during a week's sport: while the other rods had scarcely any sport worthy of the name.

Bait-fishing may be most successfully practised in the east corner of the lake where the water shallows somewhat, and the bottom weeds are not very dense. I have marked the spot which I recommend with the letter A on the plan.

There is another form of fishing which may be practised in Naukuchia, and for your teacher in this sport you can have no better guide than old Izaak Walton himself, where he describes how to dape for the chub.

"Get two or three grasshoppers as you go over the meadow; and get secretly behind the tree and stand as free from motion as is possible. Then put a grasshopper on your hook, and let your hook hang a quarter of a yard short of the water, to which end you must rest your rod on some bough of the tree. But it is likely the chubs will sink down towards the bottom of the water at the first shadow of your rod (for the chub is the fearfulest of fishes), and will do so if but a bird flies over him and makes the least shadow on the water. But they will presently rise up to the top again, and there be soaring until some shadow affrights them again. I say when they lie upon the top of the water, look out the best chub (which you setting yourself in a fit place, may very easily see) and move your rod as softly as a snail moves to that chub you intend to catch; let your bait fall gently upon the water three or four inches before him, and he will infallibly take the bait."

Nâukuchia is the only one of the Kumaun lakes in which 'daping' or 'dabbing' can be practised easily and successfully. The banks are not too steep for a quiet stalk up to an overhanging bush or tree; the fish are fond of 'soaring' under the deep shade of the boughs; and they watch keenly for any insect that may drop from its perch above.

Also the sport has this extra recommendation that it may be indulged in during the hottest part of the day, when no fish with any self-respect will move a foot after an artificial fly. Therefore, as it is now high noon, "Go your way presently, take my rod, and do as I bid you; and I will sit down and mend my tackling till you return back." But stay, my rod is far too long and too heavy for this sort of work; take this ringal nine feet long, and don't trouble yourself about a reel and running line—attach to its point a piece of line and gut together not longer than the ringal; roll up the line and gut on the point of the ringal, and having fixed your grasshopper on the hook, make your stalk on your hands and knees, as if you were bent on a shot at a wary Sambhar on a hill side. Push the ringal cautiously through the bushes till its point overhangs a clear bit of water; wait patiently while you can count two hundred, then uncurl the line so that the hook baited with the grasshopper may touch the water lightly. Doubtless you will hook something; if it be a goodly lake-fish or mahsir, throw your ringal bodily after him into the water; it will swim like a cork float, and you can by-and-bye recover rod and fish from the boat.

Nothing can exceed the beauty of the deep bays of Naukuchia lake. Time would fail me if I were to enlarge on all the sweet pictures of still-life that meet the eye of a lover of nature at every turn. Let the fishing be good, bad, or indifferent, the scenery is such as to make the heart swell with thankfulness for the opportunity and the capacity to enjoy it. And while you have been slowly wending your solitary way round the lake, now rousing yourself to add one more lusty mahsir to the half dozen already in your basket, now stopping to watch the changes of light and shade on the surrounding hills, evening has closed, and you will most likely find yourself at the point B on the plan, with a long stretch of water unfished on the south-west side of the lake. Great trees overhang the now gloomy water, and a tangled fringe of copse forms a dense undergrowth along the edge of the shore. Your heart sinks within you at the idea of fly-fishing along that bristling margin, but this is the time when you may expect the big fish to move. Make up your mind to have your cast hung up on the overhanging boughs of an acacia, and once and again to throw your fly into the spiny arms of a dog-rose, but stick to your sport till night has quenched the last faint yellow light on the western horizon.

When the bats begin to wheel round you, and to hunt your circling fly as you make your cast; when the night-jar salutes you with its monotonous "tyook-tyook;" and the big horned owl startles you with his loud human hoot from the thicket, then is the time to shift your "Silver Doctor" or "Yellow Spider" on to the thickest gut on your casting line, and gliding ghost-like along the dim wooded banks to listen for the flop of the big fish that is destined to appear shortly on your camp dinner table.

It requires a little practice and some experience to judge of distance in the gloom of evening, but it is surprising how soon the eye gets accustomed to the varying depths of shadow, and can guide the boatman as to the distance from the bushes at which he must work his boat. In my experience the men will always keep too far off if allowed: they hate the trouble of clearing a hung-up hook in the dark. Even my skilful henchman, old "Soorwa," companion of my fishing trips for a quarter of a century, has yet to receive many a whispered rating against keeping his boat too much in the deep water. You should fish with your line shortened to no more than two lengths of your rod, and after every cast draw your fly slowly and methodically towards you. Avoid anything like a sudden jerk in making a fresh cast, for at the very moment which you choose for a sharp jerk, a 5-lb. or it may be a 9-lb. fish has got your fly in his mouth, and has turned himself half round to retreat, and the chances are many that your top joint will be smashed.

But the heavy dew begins to fall, and the gusts off the high hills strike chilly along the lake; you can see the lantern gleaming across the water from the landing-place, and the fish are rising at longer intervals; reel up then and pull for your beacon light, and make haste to the cheerful shelter of your little tent, and may your bed, "more safe than soft, yield quiet sleeps."

On rare occasions morning fishing on Naukuchia is profitable, but for the most part you will find the surface of the water still and glassy till 10 o'clock, when a breeze from the east generally springs up.

To give an idea of the kind of sport to be had on this lake, I will quote from my Diary the results of two visits. In 1885 I spent a week in June on Naukuchia; the first evening I caught 12 fish, no fish over 1 lb. in weight, and the average over ¾ lb. The second day I landed six fish in the morning, three fish during an hour's fishing at 2 P. M., one of them a 5-lb. fish, and ten more in the evening, average weight a little less than 1 lb. The third day I caught nothing in the morning, but brought seven fish home in the evening. On the fourth day, I went for a walk in the morning, but in the evening landed 8 fish, all of which but two were lake-fish. On the fifth day I fished for two hours in the morning, but bagged nothing: the same evening, however, I landed nine fish; two of them mahsir, 9 lbs. and 2 lbs. The sixth day was troubled by a dust-storm and much lightning, so that with difficulty I bagged two small fish in the evening.

Again, in the middle of September 1886, I spent five days on the banks of this lovely lake. On the evening of the first day I landed seven fish, one being a mahsir of 23 lbs. weight, killed on a gold fly-spoon. Next morning there was a breeze on the lake, and I was fortunate in killing with the fly eleven fine lake-fish which scaled 13 lbs. In the evening I caught five fish of the same size. Next day fishing morning and evening, I landed only seven fish of mackarel size. On the fourth day I had ten fish, and on the fifth day ten fish.

CHAPTER V.

MALWA-TAL.

"So wondrous wild the whole might seem,
The scenery of a fairy dream."

LEAVING your camp at Naukuchia before the morning sun has surmounted the hill above Mahr-gaon, you will wend your way up the dry bed of a torrent until you reach the road leading from Bhim-tal to Malwa-tal, near the village of Padani. After a stiff climb, you will find yourself on an oak-covered ridge, whose slopes and gullies descend to the deep valley in which flows the Kalsa river. Above Janglia village, there is a lovely spot for a camp in May or June at a height of about 6,400 feet above the sea. There are green slopes of sward and shady oak glades and purling brooks of clear cold water: and were you under the guidance of Venator, instead of being the pupil of some men that what was good for me and my servants could not be bad for them and theirs; so that it became more frequented. Still at intervals frightful examples are made of some visitors, simply because they will forget that they are living in a narrow Himalayan valley not more than 3,400 feet above the sea-level, scorched by a tropical sun during the day, which bakes them between boundary cliffs 8,000 feet high, and chilled by cold winds and heavy dews in the evening and at night. If you, my friend, will make it a point to leave the lake for the shelter of the bungalow at 11 A. M., and will refrain from fishing till 3 P. M.; if you will put on a light cover coat as soon as the sun leaves the water, *however warm you may fancy it to be*, and above all, if you will content yourself with tea and coffee and water as your beverages, you will not have to complain of the climate of Malwa-tal.

As I have described at Bhim-tal, so in the Malwa-tal valley a strong breeze generally blows up the lake during the day and down the lake during the night; so that with open doors the bungalow is pleasantly cool in the hottest months. I have frequently noted the maximum temperature in the hot months, and found it to be from 82° F. to 86° F. during the day, and 72° F. to 78° F. during the night.

plateau of green sward worthy of the pleasant lawns of England;

> "I knew you young and love you now
> O shining grass and shady bough!"

and there, if you have brought a small tent with you, you will find a lovely camping ground about 150 feet above the lake.

At your feet in the north-west angle of the lake you will mark a magnificent pipul tree—welcome shade for your pony and his attendant, and close to the pipul an old temple sacred to the genius of the lake, from the door of which the old priest sees stretched at his feet a carpet of the sacred lotus lilies which fill up completely this arm of the lake. From the village of Sirori on the slopes above the temple, the sounds of shrill female voices will be heard, and by and by the Padan of the village will appear to take stock of the Sahib, and gauge through many small details whether any little attention in the shape of a lota-full of milk or a bunch of plantains or a sweet smelling cucumber — will produce a return in current coin or a rude repulse. Accept his attentions and pay him quadruple the value of his gift, but do not cultivate his acquaintance farther, for the Kumauni of the outer hills, so far as I understand him, is a poor creature, with all nobility of sentiment and of thought utterly crushed out of him.

The greatest length of Naukuchia is said to be 3,120 feet, and its widest part 2,270 feet; its approximate elevation above the sea is 4,000 feet, and its greatest depth 132 feet.

From arrangements lately made by the Assistant Commissioner of the Bhabar District, I think it is likely that a boat will be now permanently located on Naukuchia lake; but as none of the villagers about can as yet handle a scull, it will be best to arrange either with the Superintendent of the Irrigation Works who generally resides at Bhim-tal, or by writing beforehand to the Assistant Commissioner of the Bhabar District, at Naini-tal, to secure the use of a boat and of a competent boatman. As there are several boats on Bhim-tal, there will usually be no difficulty in making this arrangement.

If you have come up on your holiday without the means of camping out, you can still enjoy a day's fishing on Naukuchia by riding over early from Bhim-tal, having breakfast sent after you by a cooly, and returning in the evening by the light of one of Mr. Knaust's invaluable lanterns. But as it is far more enjoyable to camp at the lake, I recommend you to bring your Kabul tent and a shelter for your servants. The dew falls very

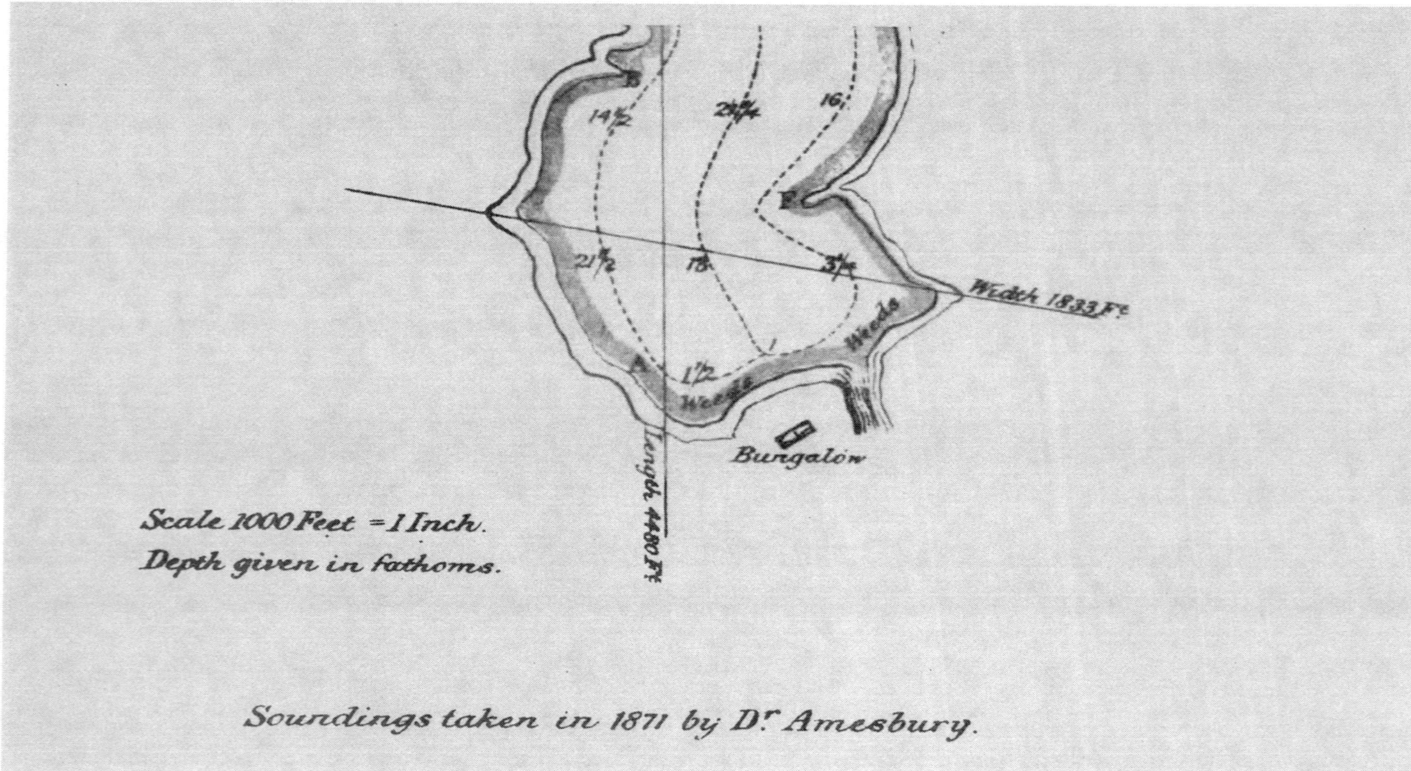
14½
24¾
16
21½
18
3¼
1½
1
Weeds
Weeds
Width 1833 Ft
Length 4480 Ft
Bungalow
Scale 1000 Feet = 1 Inch.
Depth given in fathoms.
Soundings taken in 1871 by Dr Amesbury.

MALWA-TAL.

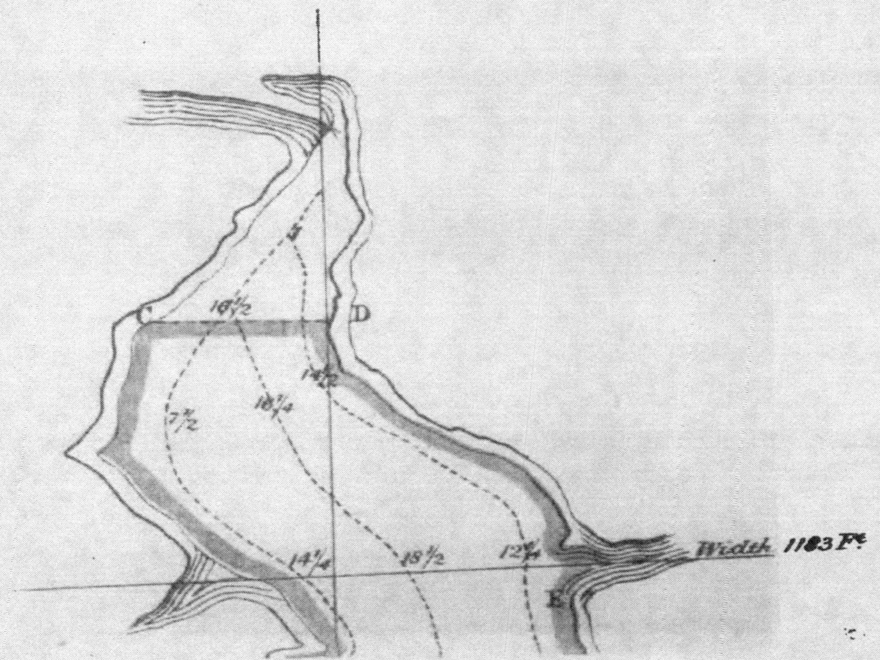

The dimensions of Malwa-tal are recorded as 4,480 feet in maximum length, 1,833 in width, and 127 feet at its deepest part; but every year these dimensions are being encroached upon. I am afraid to enter into a discussion of the origin of this lake; it looks uncommonly like a long deep pool in the Kalsa river, a sort of small Himalayan Geneva: but whatever may have been the origin of the obstruction which holds back the water at the east end of the valley, there are the clearest indications to any one who has known the lake for some years that its bed is being slowly filled up by the shingle and boulders and mud which the Kalsa and the storm torrents of the lateral gullies bring down; and that before many generations have passed away, the river will flow through the valley with scarcely a resting place for its waters.

The villagers who inhabit the houses at the east end of the valley have a tradition of a vast landslip having, many generations ago, overwhelmed the old village and formed the lake. They tell the story of an aged *fakir* being inhospitably refused food and rest by the community of the village; while having his wants supplied by an outcaste Dom and his wife. On leaving, he advised the pair to accompany him up the mountain to the site of a small temple, which is seen overhanging the lake, telling them that thus only could they escape the destruction about to fall upon the village. They took the old man's advice, and awoke in the night to hear the rush and crash of the hillside on the doomed village. In the Gazetteer of the N. W. P. will be found a nastier story of the sin which called down the wrath of the gods on the village of Malwa. You can take your choice; but, alas! for both the stories! one of those logical fellows comes along with note-book and pencil, and addresses you with a severe frown, "I have already dwelt on the point that banks of shingle (and fallen detritus from the side of the valley would share the same fate) do not in the Himalayan streams, be they large or small, give rise to permanent lakes."—I should like to cling to the village story of weak humanity and the wrath of the gods; but we had better go a-fishing, and leave him to his note-book and his logic, lest a worse thing befal us.

As the sun is still high, we will first take a good look at the lake as we sit in the verandah of the bungalow. The strike of the valley is north-west and south-east. Before the embankment was swept away in the floods of 1880, the water used to be held up so as to cover the wide expanse of shingle now seen at the north-west end, and filled up entirely the narrow valley, until the lake disappeared round the furthest projecting spur of the north-west boundary. The hills enclosing the valley rise in picturesque grandeur, some 3,000 feet above the level of the lake. On the north-west side the cliffs are precipitous, and are seamed with gullies, down which, in the rainy season, huge detached masses of rock are heard plunging and crashing into the shingly and pine-covered slopes below. On the south-east side the hills are equally lofty, but less precipitous, more wooded and retiring further back as they ascend, until their topmost peaks form the oak and rhododendra-covered slopes which we admired above Janglia.

Shutting up the valley to the west is a wall of mountain, pine-covered on its sides and with a bristling fringe of tall pines cutting the sky line.

> 'Higher yet, the pine tree hung
> His shattered trunk, and frequent flung,
> Where seemed the cliffs to meet on high,
> His boughs athwart the narrow sky.'

In the days I speak of, Malwa-tal, washing the feet of those stupendous mountains, and disappearing mysteriously under the pine-covered wall of rock to the westward, impressed the imagination with a gloomy vastness that cannot now be conjured up in view of the shingle bed lying white and glistening at its western end. It is still beautiful with the beauty of grand surroundings, but it has lost its infinite mystery.

Before taking to your boat, you may try a cast in the stream as it issues from the lake: there are always a number of small mahsir hanging about and considerable shoals of trout. Once embarked in your boat, you will find the shallow water in front of the outlet of the lake swarming with year old mahsir, with here and there a solid 2-lb. fish in their company; but you had better leave this bit of water unfished till your return at dusk. Get at once into the shadows on the west side of the lake, and fish quietly round as I have already advised. The claret-bodied fly with the mixed wing, and the golden pheasant topping tail you will find most killing on this lake; at all events while the day is bright and the sun high. There is a steep cliff marked A on the plan about fifty yards from the south-west corner of the lake, where I have bagged many a good fish. The rock is pretty clear of grass and bushes, and you will have little difficulty in landing your fly on bare portions of it, so as to let it drop from the rock on to the water. The instant it touches the water you will have a rise, and if you have profited by the lessons of Bhim-tal and Naukuchia, you will hook and land your fish without trouble. From A to B there is deep water, and

I have had good sport in this reach along the thickly wooded bank. You will often see large fish moving lazily about near the surface, crossing your path or coming towards you—taking an afternoon stroll as it were. While, therefore, making your casts steadily under the bushes, and amongst the long grass at the edge of the lake, keep your eye on the water ahead of you, and stop the boat by a motion of your hand when you see one of the brown shadows moving in your direction: wait quietly till he comes within range of your cast; kneel down in the boat and drop your fly deftly about a foot in front of him; it is ten chances to one that he will launch himself forward with a sweep of his broad tail, and be hooked almost as soon as the fly begins to move to the rising point of your rod.

There is one serious danger to be overcome in this bay, and, indeed, more or less round all the shores of Malwa- and Sath-tals, namely, the presence of sunken trees. Heat and moisture favor the rapid growth of soft-wooded tall trees on the steep banks of the lake, and these frequently topple over, and their tangled boughs, preserved under the water, remain for many years a glorious sanctuary for a stricken fish. One evening at the west end of this lake a tree, at least 40 feet in height with a magnificent head of branches, fell without any warning into the water not more than twenty yards from the spot where I was intently fishing. If, therefore, you hook a fish near one of those sunken trees, hold him hard and give him no law. From the promontory at B all along the south-east side of the lake till you reach the shingle bank at the west end there is good fishing, the size of the fish mostly like mackerel, with now and again a 3-lb. to 5-lb. fish to help up the average. The plan of the lake and the soundings which I have given were made in 1871; since that date the process of filling up has gone on apace, until now the dotted line drawn between C and D would roughly represent the western shore. Along this steep sloping bank of shingle you will see thousands of young mahsir, and here and there will mark the shadowy outline of a great fish. When the Kalsa river is in flood, spinning at the mouth of the stream, either with a leaded gold spoon or with dead bait, is sometimes very successful, although the fish are easily alarmed, and you will not secure more than one or two at a single visit. The best time of the day for this sport is just as the sun strikes the stream in the morning. I have myself landed several 10-lb. fish under those circumstances; and I am aware of a 30-lb. fish having been killed, in 1886, at this spot.

Early one morning after heavy rain over the

catchment area of the Kalsa, I found the river tearing through the clear water of the lake for 200 yards in a wide, clay-colored torrent, which, passing along the bottom, appeared an hour later at the outlet of the lake, leaving for many hours the intervening water and the side bays as clear as usual. On the edge of the flood water, hanging on the skirts of the floating rubbish brought down by the river, I found shoals of large mahsir feeding eagerly, and I never had a more exciting two hours' sport. I have no doubt, therefore, that on rare and special occasions the best sport to be had on any of the Kumaun lakes, may be obtained at the entrance of the Kalsa into Malwa-tal.

Off the bank of shingle I have been told that excellent ground-bait fishing can be had, but I have never tried it.

Returning by the western shore you will find the best sport under the high trees that overhang the water in the reach between E and F on the plan; while a most promising spot for evening fishing is the promontory at F. Then as night closes, putting on the yellow spider and using stronger tackle, you may boldly venture among the fish which swarm in the east end of the lake and round the outlet.

To give the reader an idea of the kind of sport to be had on Malwa-tal I make an extract from my Diary:—On the 17th June 1879 I reached the lake at 10 A.M. Heavy thunder showers, precursors of the monsoon, fell during the day but it cleared about 4 P.M. Before dark, I killed thirty fish with the fly, on fine trout tackle; these fish scaled 40 lbs. Next morning (the 18th) was fine, and I secured 12 fish of mackerel size. In the evening I brought in 43 fish of average size; I did not weigh them. On the 19th, I had 28 fish, and on the 20th, 20 fish in the morning, one of 5 lbs., and 23 average-sized fish in the evening.

There can be no doubt that there are in Malwatal some very old and very large mahsir; but they are thinned out every year by being tempted to run up the Kalsa and down the Gola when these rivers are in flood. The floods rapidly subside, and the fish are then seen in the clear pools, and become an easy prey to the devices of the country gentlemen. On several occasions when the lake has been discolored by rain or by infusoria, I have seen huge fish come close to my boat following the struggles of a hooked fish. A good many years ago I recollect a 21-lb. fish being landed on fine tackle by a good fisherman, Col. D., and lately I have heard of two heavy fish scaling close on 30 lbs. each being caught, one by spinning a dead bait at the mouth of the Kalsa, and the other (tell it not in Gath!) by a trimmer set at night.

There are two drawbacks to sport on Malwa-tal: it is undoubtedly a hot valley to fish in, and good drinking water is procured with difficulty. As regards the latter, I have been in the habit of sending for it to the springs on the hill above Janglia: but there is also a good spring above Malwa village under the steep scarp of the south-eastern boundary of the valley. As for the valley being particularly unhealthy and malarious, one has only to study the appearance of the men and women living in the village to see that they are not malaria stricken: and, as a matter of fact, I have known individual inhabitants of the village for the past sixteen years who have maintained robust health although rarely leaving the valley.

Otters abound on this lake. I have seen five and six at one time fishing together: but they will seldom give you a chance of adding to your peltry. I have carried a rifle often with me while fishing, but never once secured a reasonably fair shot. One morning when getting into my boat, I came very near to having a shot! I noticed a movement amongst some well-grown rice on the sloping bank at the east end of the lake. Presently two full grown otters glided into the water. I snatched up my Express, and watched for a 'vent.' One otter swam straight away to the middle of the lake, the second turned sharp, not having seen the boat, and from the air bubbles breaking on the surface, I could see him coming towards us in a bee line. Without once giving 'vent' he passed under the boat, bumping his head on the bottom, took his breath, gave an angry snarl at a native who was sitting on the bank holding on to the 'painter,' and again diving passed away into deep water without once offering a shot. One evening an otter rose close to my boat with a large water snake in his mouth: he looked me calmly in the face, swam ashore and walked away up through the bushes as if he had never seen a human being before, and did not believe in the invention of gunpowder.

There is always a pair of fish hawks on Malwa-tal, and the same may be said of Bhim-tal, Nau-kuchia and Sath-tal. I have never seen more than one pair at a time, and conclude that they do not brook rivals on their hunting grounds. The two birds generally perch far apart on dead stumps of trees, and as your boat approaches, they fly off to another coign of vantage, with a clanging cry that rouses the echoes.

The jungle round Malwa valley is dense enough to give cover to the most timid and wary of wild animals. You will frequently see goral drinking in midday at the edge of the lake. I have seen a sounder of wild pig cooling themselves by a swim across the lake at high noon. Young serao have been brought to me by the villagers. Towards October you will hear jerao belling at night in the dense thickets: they are not numerous, but a few are always present: and I have been startled uncommonly in the dusk by a stag dashing up the hill-side from the margin of the lake where he had been drinking and watching curiously the approach of the silent boat. Altogether, although I cannot commend Malwa-tal as a suitable spot for a jaded angler from the plains in which to regain strength and vigour, it is without doubt a most pleasant spot, in which a man in good health may spend a week or ten days with great satisfaction. He can vary sport on the lake by long strolls over the hills with a light single-barrelled rifle, and he will find rest and quiet and time for thought—luxuries which alas! modern life in India has almost banished from its menu.

CHAPTER VI.

SATH-TAL.

SATH-TAL, "the seven lakes," are thus described in Mr. Atkinson's volume of the N. W. P. Gazetteers :—

"A collection of lakes in Pargannah Chhakhata of the Kumaun District, about nine miles from Naini-tal, *turning off from the Ramgar road at Bhuwali*, and three miles from Bhim-tal. They are the *most picturesque, if not the grandest*, of the lakes of this district. They *are formed of landslips* in the basin of the range in which they lie. The first lake met with is a deep black tarn, wooded to the water's edge, and *connected by an underground passage* with the fourth. Passing further into the basin a second very small pool is met with close to the third at the irrigation embankment : thence the path winds round the third to the fourth, which is the largest, and is a very considerable sheet of water about 1,100 yards in length by 350 in breadth. *All three larger ones communicate with each other*, and the water level has been raised considerably by the embankment which makes these lakes a reservoir for the supply of water to the Bhabur during the dry season from February onwards. Below the embankment to the south is another small lake, the fifth : and beyond this in the bed of the stream, two lakes now dried up : hence the name of 'Sath-tal' or seven lakes."

I have printed in italics certain statements in the above description to which I feel called upon to take exception. Acknowledging as I willingly do the general accuracy of the facts and descriptions recorded in Mr. Atkinson's volume, I feel assured that he will be the last man to object to the correction of mistakes which seem to have arisen from incorrect information supplied to him. I cannot believe that the statements to which I take exception were made after a personal inspection of the seven lakes by the author himself. Certainly Mr. Atkinson could never have reached Sath-tal "by turning off the Ramgar road at Bhuwali." The pathway to the seven lakes leaves the Bhim-tal valley road fully a mile after passing the Bhuwali stream at the foot of the second steep descent, where a small perennial irrigation streamlet crosses the road. It is by no means easy to find this path, as the district authorities have never made any attempt to construct a bridle road from the Bhim-tal road to Sath-tal.

It is of course a mere matter of opinion whether these lakes 'are the most picturesque, if not the grandest,' of the Kumaun lakes: my opinion will be found further on in these pages, but I cannot pass over without remark the unqualified conclusion that the 'seven lakes' "are formed by landslips in the basin of the range in which they lie." Mr. Theobald has, in his paper published in Part 3 of Vol. XIII of the Records of the Geological Survey, given abundant reasons to prove that the barrier which has formed the three large lakes (the others are of no moment) cannot be anything but the remains of the moraine of a glacier which "crept down from almost due north till arrested by the hill whereon Siloti stands." Overlooking the odium geologicum, which permeates and taints Mr. Theobald's paper, his conclusions are, I think, sound, and that it is not possible to conceive a barrier formed by a landslip in a Himalayan valley being able to hold back permanently the waters of a lake.

But I pass on to other even more serious mistakes into which Mr. Atkinson has been led. He describes the first lake as being "connected by an underground passage with the fourth," that is with the largest of the lakes. He evidently is not aware that the first lake, 'his deep black tarn,' is situated 175 feet above the fourth lake, and that, as it is only 80 feet deep, it is difficult to conceive how the water can remain in it and rise and fall independently with the seasons, were there any underground communication between the lakes. The difference between low water and flood-level in the third and fourth lakes is 30 feet: the difference between the summer and monsoon level of the upper lake is only 15 feet.

There is, I may note, a leak from the upper lake, which appears in the form of a spring by the side of the pathway half-way between the upper and the embanked lakes; but the outflow is insignificant, is uniform at all seasons, and finds its way not into the large lakes, but into the ravine to the south of the embankment.

I think, therefore, we may conclude that there is no underground communication between the first and fourth lakes, neither is there any junction between the third and fourth, except through the narrow channel cut artificially between the two lakes. For in 1886 the artificial cutting was allowed to silt up, and until it had been cleaned out and deepened, the water in the fourth or largest lake stood five feet higher than the water-level in the third or embankment lake. This could not have occurred had there been any other communication between these lakes.

Sath-tal may be reached from Bhim-tal by

keeping the bridle-road leading to the Bhim-tal tea gardens, passing through the gardens and so on to the ridge where the pathway from the Bhuwali side meets the private garden road. From the ridge the path dips at once into the valley of the seven lakes. About one hundred yards below the ridge there is a fine open grassy slope for encamping, and good drinking water is close at hand on the Bhim-tal side of the dividing ridge. To fish Sath-tal properly you must live near the lakes, and until the last year (1887) the only way to do so was to pitch a small tent on the slope of the hill. Now, however, thanks to the energy and enterprise of Mr. Jones, Proprietor of the Bhim-tal Tea Gardens, there are two double storied chalets for rent, furnished and equipped similarly to the single storied chalet at Bhim-tal, and to be hired at rents of Rs. 60 and Rs. 70 respectively for the whole chalet, or of Rs. 35 and Rs. 40 for one-half. Each half is complete in itself and has a small separate kitchen, which renders it possible for two parties to live in each chalet comfortably.

As an angler you need not trouble yourself to visit any but the two large lakes (the third and fourth of Mr. Atkinson's description). In the first lake, the gloomy black pool which lies below you to your left as you descend into the valley, there

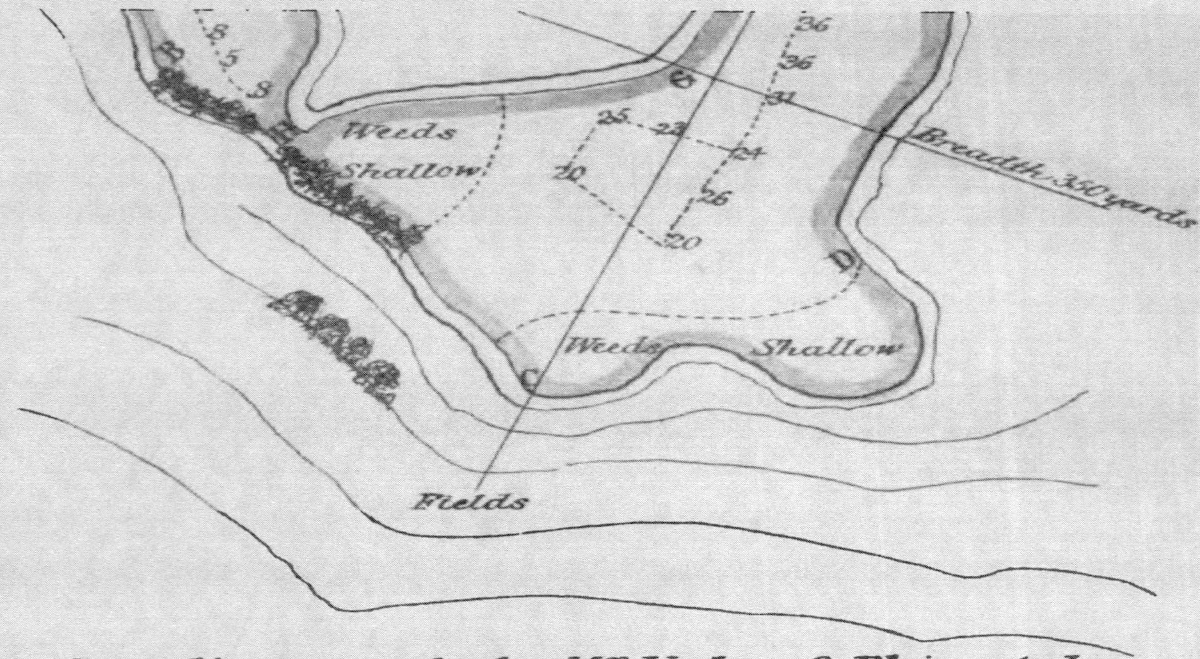

Soundings made by Mr. Yule of Bhim-tal.

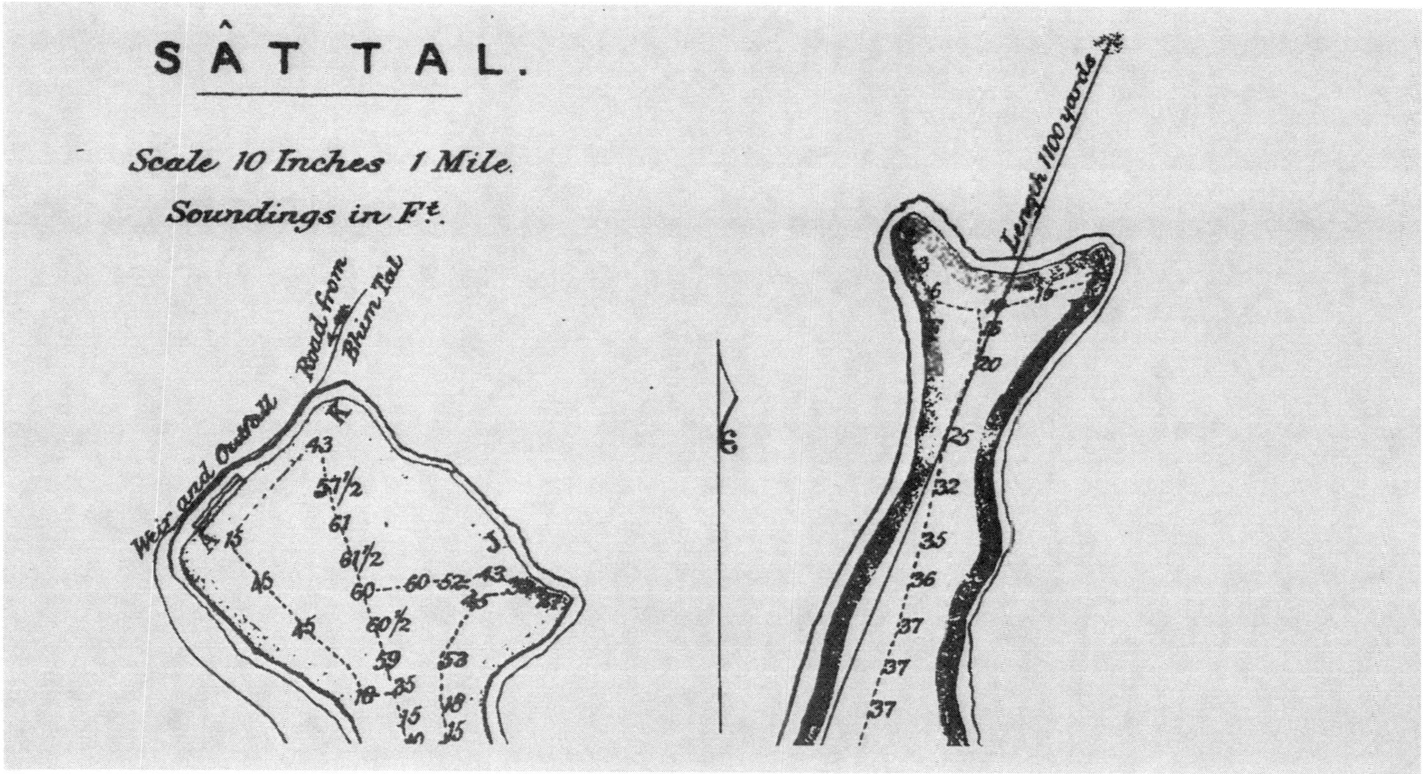
SÂT TAL.
Scale 10 Inches 1 Mile.
Soundings in Ft.
Road from Bhim Tal
Weir and Outfall
Length 1100 yards

are, I believe, no fish. This is the report of the natives, and although I have often watched the surface of this tarn from the slope above, where my tent was pitched, I have never seen a rise on it. I have watched a small species of coot playing on its surface, and I have seen large water snakes threading their sinuous way hither and thither, but fish I have never seen; and if there are any, they must be very small and entirely ground-feeders.

Passing this upper lake the pathway leads you on to the embankment and weir at the north-west extremity of the smaller of the two large lakes, and there you will find your boat moored, if you have taken the precaution to communicate beforehand with the Assistant Superintendent of the Bhabar District at Naini-tal and had orders sent to Mr. J. Docherty, Supervisor of Irrigation Works, Bhim-tal, to send a boat over in anticipation of your arrival. If you are in any difficulty for a boatman, there is an old fellow, a Lohar, who lives in the village which you will find nestling at the northern end of the large lake, who can manage a boat fairly well. His son also is accustomed to handle the sculls.

Having got afloat begin fishing at the weir, and if the sun is passing westward of the meridian, keep along the west side of the smaller lake.

From A to B you will find many lake-fish (B. chilinoides) lying and willing to rise to a well thrown fly, but you will not see many mahsir. And just as in Naukuchia I have found the fish to be keen after the 'Silver Doctor,' so on Sath-tal, for day fishing, I have noticed that the fish have a decided preference for a fly with a claret body and mallard wing which I have made an attempt to describe below :—

Tag silver thread: but orange silk: tail a few mixed fibres of mallard and golden pheasant tippet: body claret colored pig's wool: claret hackle rather full: silver tinsel: wings strips of mallard and golden pheasant tippet: head black.

From the point marked B on the west shore you will find the banks lined with thorn and rose bushes and the water comparatively shallow. I have here often had good sport with small fish. In the narrow channel which joins the two lakes when the weir is closed, you will generally find some fair sized mahsir on the look-out for food; in this spot I hooked and landed after some trouble on light tackle a six-pound fish. When the lakes are low, that is any time between March and July, the passage between them is only navigable through the winding artificial cut made to admit the water of the large lake into the embankment lake. From this narrow channel all along the western and southern shores of the large lake the ground is much the same as between B and the Straits. There is a well defined bank, with overshadowing bushes and low trees, but it depends on the height of the water in the lake whether the sloping foreshore will be covered with water and to what extent. If you have hit off the season when the water is rising after the first closing of the weir, you will find large numbers of fish feeding on the newly covered grass banks, and will also find them eager for the fly. Don't neglect the shallow corner of the lake at D, for it has yielded not a few good fish for my basket; but, as the water is shallow, the cast must be approached with great caution, stooping or sitting down in your boat, throwing a long line, and giving the fish no opportunity to warn his comrades when you have hooked him.

But in my experience the very best of the water on Sath-tal lies along the east shore of the large lake. It is without doubt the most difficult part of the lake to fish properly, but it will repay care and trouble a hundredfold. The banks are steep and wooded to the edge of the water, a fringe of long grass and wild flowers droops over the margin, and under this glorious shade the fish lie in wait. You may often hear them close under the bank flapping their tails, and shaking the stems of the grass in their attempts to dislodge an unwary beetle or grasshopper from his perch.

My observation has led me to conclude that the mahsir are not fond of this side of the lake. I have caught them now and again; but the fish which yields the sport along this shore is the chilinoides. In none of the lakes will you secure so many and so large fish of this species as in Sath-tal. I have records in my diary of several takes in which the average weight of two dozen fish was over one pound. One great charm of the fishing along this eastern shore is its difficulty, and the dangers to which your tackle is exposed. You will come upon overturned sunken trees dead for years under the water, and trees half dead standing erect covered with misletoe and other parasites at varying distances of from 8 to 20 feet from the shore line, and in dealing with an active fish you have to calculate the bearings and position of each of those obstacles before you can venture to give him his head in any direction. Surrounded as the fish are by most prolific vegetation, they are greedy insect feeders, are constantly on the watch for their prey, and being so much on the move, they are active and in prime condition. I venture, however, to warn you again that, eager as they may be to feed, you are not dealing with unsophisticated fish. If you wish to make a really good bag, you must fish throughout with care; and it is surprising how soou you will find yourself recognizing many of the casts that would pass muster very well on a Scotch stream to be utter bungling when made over a lake mahsir or black-fish. I have now fished for many years on the Kumaun lakes, and begin to flatter myself that I can throw a fly fairly well under a 'Gingaroo' bush; and yet after an hour's fishing, I am forced to confess that no wide-a-wake fish would think of rising to three out of five of my casts. As the day wears on the wrist gets tired, the attention begins to flag, you will cease to be able to direct your fly to the exact spot on which it must alight, if the fish is to be tempted from his hold: you have reached the witching hour "tween the gloamin and the mirk when the kye comes hame," therefore, my friend, reel up and rest for a while on the bosom of the lake.

There is solitude and quiet beauty about Sath-tal but no grandeur. The vegetation clothing the sides of the valley is for the most part very dense. You will notice many lovely orchids depending from the branches of the trees, and the evening air will be loaded with the aromatic scent of the flowers of many climbing plants that riot among their boughs; you will come upon a bed of graceful white lilies, and wish you could carry them all away with you; but you will be disappointed if you expect grandeur of scenery. The lake is shut in on all sides by low forest covered hills; it is a rare thing to see the water lit up by the sun in a brisk breeze; the higher ranges are completely shut out, while the hills immediately enclosing the valley are neither precipitous nor lofty, like those which overhang the waters of Malwa. In my opinion Sath-tal cannot be compared for beauty to Naukuchia or even to Bhim-tal when its waters are at flood-level. Like all deep narrow gorges in the Himalayas the valley is remarkable for intense pungent heat during the day, and for equally sharp damp cold at night. If, therefore, you fish late, it is absolutely necessary to put on an overcoat after dusk, and to make your boatman draw his blanket hood-fashion over his head and shoulders, if you and he wish to avoid a chill, and a probable attack of fever which will stop your fishing for many days.

But however diverse opinions may be as to the beauty of the scenery in Sath-tal, the angler cannot fail to find that most precious of boons in this hurrying, bustling modern life—quiet and solitude :—

"Dear Solitude! the soul's best friend,
That man acquainted with himself dost make
And all his Maker's wonders to intend,
With thee, I here converse at will,
And would be glad to do so still
For it is thou alone that keep'st the soul awake."

You will find the two corners of the northern end of the large lake shallow and encumbered not only with weeds, but with overhanging boughs of trees and undergrowth; but still they are worthy of being carefully fished, for they often hold large mahsir in search for change of diet. There is much glorious excitement to be had in our lake-fishing, but there is nothing that equals the sharp sudden call upon your skill and resource in dealing with a big fish on fine tackle when surrounded by weeds and snags, with only one hope for safety in half coaxing, half dragging him through the narrow clear central channel of a deep creek till you gain the open lake.

The bank from F to G along the west side of the large lake very much resembles that on the opposite side, but it is not so difficult to fish and does not hold so many fish. From the point G till you reach the shallow water at the junction of the two lakes mahsir are plentiful, and there is no special difficulty in bagging them. Once you have passed through the Straits, and are fairly on your way round the east bank of the smaller lake, you will notice that the rises of mahsir are more frequent; and I am quite convinced from many opportunities of observation that the favorite haunts of the mahsir in Sath-tal are along the eastern shore of the small lake, and in front of the embankment at its north-west end.

When fishing in the morning do not begin till the sun touches the water, and then reverse the course which I have recommended for an afternoon's fishing. The fish are never so keen in the morning as in the evening; early rising is not fashionable on Sath-tal; but you will hook a fish now and again from under the bushes; and if you keep your weather-eye on the still clear water ahead of your boat, you will see small groups of mahsir basking near the surface on the line between the sunshine and the shadow of the bank. It will afford you a fair test of your skill in lake-fishing if you can make a cast so as to lure one of those early risers to quit his companions and take your fly. You will rarely find any breeze on Sath-tal till about 10 A. M., and then it will be partial and only in cap-fuls.

If you care for ground-bait fishing, I have heard of good sport being had off the embankment. I am also aware of an 18-lb. fish having been taken on a deeply trolled spoon bait. But you may take my word for it, that in using the fly, you will not only have far more genuine sport than from any other form of angling, but you will, in the end, over a number of days secure a far greater weight of fish.

Night-fishing in warm weather, I have been told, is a very remunerative sport. Of one thing I am sure—it ought to be full of surprises and of embarrassing situations, were it not that mahsir when hooked at night are fools, and give up all the advantages of home defence out of pure curiosity to find out what sort of insect is leading them by the nose into deep water. For night-fishing, I would recommend the yellow spider or any large lightish colored fly in your book; failing those, a tag of a bathing towel will probably answer the purpose!

The public are indebted to Sir Henry Ramsay for the mahsir fishing in the Kumaun lakes. On account of the steep falls at or below the outlets of all the lakes, except Malwa-tal, no mahsir could possibly have got unaided into them. Into Malwa-tal it is possible that fish could get at most seasons from the Gola river.

About thirty years ago Sir H. Ramsay had some small mahsir carried up from the Gola in earthenware *ghurras* to stock Bhim-tal, Naukuchia, and Sath-tal, and from the Kosi river to stock Naini-tal.

These young fish prospered in Naini-tal, in Sath-tal and in Naukuchia, but they failed in Bhim-tal. For up to 1873 I never saw nor heard of a mahsir being caught in Bhim-tal.

Later however (I think in 1878), Sir H. Ramsay

again made an effort to introduce mahsir into Bhim-tal, and this time with success. The fish are now flourishing in Bhim-tal, as well as in many of the other lakes. I have myself caught mahsir in Bhim-tal, weighing 8 lbs., and I am aware of one having been caught on a live-bait, which weighed 18 lbs.

As regards 'Kali-macchi'—'Lake fish' or 'Kurn-kutla,' I cannot get information of any period at which they did not exist in the lakes, but whether they were introduced in pre-historic times or like Topsy 'growed' there, I cannot say.

And now, brother angler, fare-thee-well. I have shared with you all the information which years of observation have enabled me to accumulate about our well loved sport on these charming lakes. I hope that "I am like to have a towardly scholar of you." But remember, as old Taylor in his 'Art of Angling' says, that "experience and observation alone can make an angler a complete adept in the art, so as to enable him to throw his fly behind bushes and trees into holes and under banks where the best fish are to be found." Even should nature and opportunity deny your ever becoming a "complete adept," still you may have infinite pleasure out of a small measure of success, and you will at least refresh your jaded soul and body with the pure air and healthful quiet of the mountain vallies, and you will be heard humming cheerfully as you enter the train at Katgodam, which will take you back to the gin-horse round of office and court-house, of orderly-room and parade ground:

> "Blest silent lakes, oh! may you be
> For ever health's best nursery!
> May pure contents
> For ever pitch their tents
> Upon these downs, these meads, these rocks, these mountains,
> And peace still slumber by these purling fountains,
> Which we may every year
> Meet when we come a fishing here."

THE END.